THE ARTS AND CRAFTS MOVEMENT IN THE LAKE DISTRICT

The Arts and Crafts Movement in the Lake District

A Social History

Jennie Brunton

Centre for North-West Regional Studies
University of Lancaster
2001
Series Editor: Jean Turnbull

The Arts and Crafts Movement in the Lake District: A Social History

This volume is the 45th in a series published by the Centre for North-West Regional Studies at the University of Lancaster

Published by the Centre for North-West Regional Studies,
University of Lancaster

Designed and typeset by Carnegie Publishing Ltd,
Carnegie House, Chatsworth Road, Lancaster LA1 4SL

Printed and bound in the UK by The Cromwell Press, Trowbridge

British Library Cataloguing-in-Publication Data
A CIP catalogue record for this book is available from the British Library

ISBN 1–86220–111–0

Contents

List of Illustrations

Acknowledgements

In the production of this book I would like to thank all those who contributed knowingly or unknowingly to its completion. I am grateful for the early support Mary Rose gave to this project and the funding of my on-going research by the Pasold Research Fund. Institutional support facilitated by my Honorary Research Associate status in the History Department at Lancaster University is also gratefully acknowledged. In carrying out my research in the archives of Cumbria I would like to record my thanks to David Bowcock and the staff at Carlisle, Richard Hall in Kendal Record Office and to Alice Pearson and the staff at Abbot Hall. Further afield I would like to thank Linda Parry for revealing some of the hidden treasures held at the Victoria & Albert Museum.

In any study of the Arts and Crafts Movement it is important to include large numbers of illustrations. I have been fortunate to gain access to images in both public and private collections. I am particularly grateful to staff at the Cumbria Record Office, Carlisle; Elizabeth Buchanan; Eleanor Davidson; the Museum of Lakeland Life, Abbot Hall; John Marsh and Stephen Wildman of the Ruskin Foundation for giving permission to include images in the book. I would also like to thank Chris Beacock of the Geography Department at Lancaster for drawing the map of the Lake District.

Contact with descendants of those involved with these industries has added a special dimension to my work and I thank both Eleanor Davidson and John Marsh for their contributions.

As with all acknowledgements I thank friends and family; particularly Jack, Kate and Chloe who have become accustomed to a distracted mother.

John Walton was kind enough to return to his old role and once more commit his pen and thoughts on my manuscript, for this I thank him. In supporting and publishing this work I thank Jacqueline Whiteside and the CNWRS. In her role as administrator, editor, and for her support surely above and beyond the call of duty, my very special thanks are extended to Jean Turnbull.

Jennie Brunton, Lancaster 2001

Foreword

The themes of this book are rooted in two and a half centuries of Lakeland history. Tourism in the Lake District had its eighteenth-century origins in the appreciation of the landscape and scenery through the conventions of the picturesque and the sublime; but visitors (increasingly drawn from urban backgrounds) and the guide-book writers who helped to direct their gaze soon became romantically drawn to the proud but humble inhabitants of these mountain fastnesses, to borrow the enduring linguistic currency in which they dealt. At the turn of the eighteenth and nineteenth century Wordsworth played an important part in peopling the landscape with an imagined virtuous peasantry, bringing the little-used word 'statesman' out of obscurity to give a distinctive regional cast to the predominant owner-occupier farmers who were usually known as the 'yeomanry', a claim to special status which was itself becoming increasingly archaic by the time the railway reached the shores of Windermere in 1847. 'Statesmen' or 'yeomen' were seen as the embodiment of old-fashioned rustic virtue. They were frugal, hardy, honest, hard-working, unpretentious and deeply rooted in their native soil; and they eked out a simple living by combining farming with domestic manufacture, especially the spinning of yarn and weaving of cloth. This was presented as a virtuous lifestyle which could rub off to the moral benefit of the visitors, who were assumed to come from more sophisticated (in the pejorative sense) urban environments in which commerce, fashion and emergent consumerism had rendered such a 'natural' way of life unfortunately obsolete.

But the imagined way of life of the Lakeland 'yeoman' or 'statesman' was visibly under threat by the mid-nineteenth century, as tourism helped to import new fashions and aspirations, and new ways of making money (not least by selling land for development), while the markets for the domestic crafts withered and died. Not everyone regretted the changes: Harriet Martineau, in a Lake District guide-book of 1855, offered a different reading of the rustic inhabitants as ignorant, clownish, drunken, dirty and potentially violent, and rejoiced at the spread of shops, hotels, hot baths and the comforts of urban civilization through the twin agencies of the railways and the tourist trade. But this was iconoclastic. Most commentators regretted the changes; and it was this frame of mind, linking landscape with an idealized vision of the people, that sought to revive country crafts and rural virtues in the last quarter of the nineteenth century. This was part of a much wider movement, of course, with distinctive incarnations right across Europe and beyond; and in England the relationship between this frame of mind and the activities of the Arts and Crafts Movement and its engagingly eccentric and sometimes luridly outrageous proponents has been investigated in lively style by authors such as Fiona MacCarthy. What has been remarkable is the lack of such studies in a Lake District setting; and this is the gap which Jennie Brunton's thorough, crisply-written and well-documented set of case-studies begins to fill. It builds outwards from her doctoral thesis on Annie Garnett, and its cast of strong and sometimes conflicting personalities, though less outrageous than Eric Gill or even Charles Ashbee, nevertheless provides the basis for some compelling narratives. It includes, after all, Canon Hardwicke Rawnsley, whose role as watchdog of the Lakes against unsuitable innovations and developments was complemented by his efforts to revitalise 'traditional' crafts and the imagined way of life that had gone with them; and above it all broods the turbulent spirit of that other Old Man of Coniston, the Victorian sage John Ruskin. But I leave these rich and interlinked stories to the author herself, who is the person best qualified to tell them.

John K. Walton

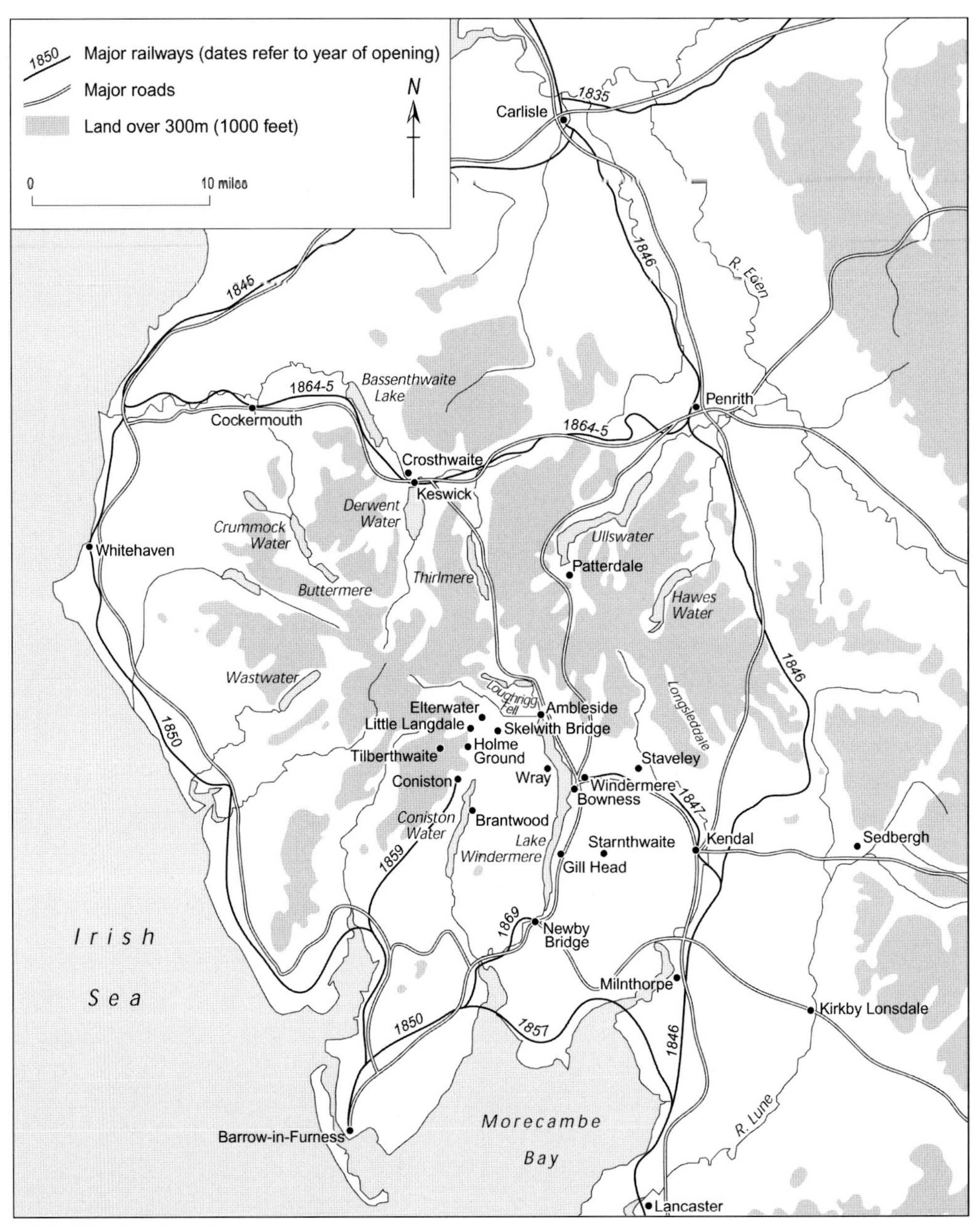

Map of the Lake District. Includes key place names for the Arts & Crafts Movement. Map drawn by Chris Beacock.

CHAPTER ONE

Introduction: Contextualising the Arts and Crafts Movement in the Lake District

> The Arts and Crafts was a metropolitan movement to the extent that the formative events in its history took place in London, and London was the home of its principal organisations and many of its leading figures. In late nineteenth-century Britain it could hardly have been otherwise. But it was not exclusively so. It flourished early and independently in South Devon, with its potteries and laceworkers, and on the banks of Lake Windermere, where the Ruskin Linen Industry was set up as early as 1883. And, as the Movement gathered its strength in the provinces in the 1890s, it was often in country areas that it was strongest, for in the imagination of the Arts and Crafts, 'the countryside' wove spells only less potent than 'the Middle Ages'. There were Arts and Crafts workshops set up to provide employment for country people, particularly by the Home Arts and Industries Association, to stem the migration to the towns; and there were others founded by migrants from the towns, sophisticated urbanites in search of the perfect rustic setting.[1]

Besides signifying the importance of London to the Arts and Crafts Movement, so named after the Society's first exhibition there in 1888, Alan Crawford also indicates the diverse and regional nature of this aesthetic and social movement. More specific to this study, however, is his identification of an industry 'on the banks of Lake Windermere' in perhaps that most 'perfect rustic setting', the English Lake District. In broadening the perspective beyond the lake to the surrounding hills this book aims to reveal and retell the history of four particular craft industries which were established at Elterwater, Kendal and Keswick, as well as Bowness in the 1880s.

Elterwater was the centre of the Langdale Linen Industry, founded by Albert Fleming and Marion Twelves, when it had its headquarters in St Martin's cottage. Kendal was home to the woodcarving and furniture-making family firm of the Simpsons, while in Keswick Harwicke Rawnsley and his wife Edith established a permanent centre for the craft classes they had begun in Wray with the Keswick School of Industrial Arts. Inspired by what she saw in Elterwater Annie Garnett set up her own linen industry at The Spinnery in Bowness, which evolved to include the manufacture of more sophisticated textiles.

Acknowledging that as a social history this book is primarily about people and their motivation, it is perhaps not surprising that the presence of John Ruskin in the area, following his purchase of Brantwood in 1871, should prove to have particular significance to many of the individuals involved. Annie Garnett wrote on hearing of his death:

> ... how much he has done to keep us in the right way will probably never be quite realised. Such a gentle influence he yielded which gathers in its fold all who read him; none can be quite the same after reading him.[2]

As the source of ideologies promulgated in such works as 'The Nature of Gothic' and *Fors Clavigera: Letters to the Workmen and Labourers of Great Britain* (1871), which espoused the artistic merits of individual craft-workers and the need to restore rural industries, his words were to have a particular local relevance and warrant some early, albeit brief, attention in this text. Ruskin's quest to inform people of the dire consequences of industrialisation did not cease when he reached his northern retreat but instead was reinforced by his daily monitoring of the skies over Coniston Water. These records as he showed in his subsequent 1884 publication, *The Storm Cloud of the Nineteenth Century*, proved prophetic in observing the polluting effects of the northern factories.

The Influential Presence of John Ruskin

Although John Ruskin was 'not alone in diagnosing his country's disease as a competitive economic philosophy'[3] he did, however, appear to occupy a unique perspective in relating his views in terms of art, society, work and religion. Ruskin's role as a social and economic commentator had evolved from his early work as an art critic, in *Modern Painters* (1843), to the point where he saw the contribution of individual creativity as a crucial component in what he would define as a civilised society. Reading Thomas Carlyle had awakened the young Ruskin to the dehumanising effects of industrialisation and the government's policy of laissez-faire. However, although Carlyle may be attributed with inspiring Ruskin to question the so-called progress of nineteenth century economic growth, a more fundamental early influence had ingrained him with

John Ruskin 1885. Photograph by Barraud, London. Ruskin Foundation (Ruskin Library, University of Lancaster).

deeply felt religious beliefs and a desire to promote a more caring hierarchical social order, as advocated in the Bible. In perceiving the moral injustice of a developing nineteenth century capitalist system, which exploited workers to bring wealth to the few, Ruskin was to invoke his Biblical knowledge to state, somewhat controversially, that if 'the poor have no right to the property of the rich, I wish it also to be known and declared that the rich have no right to the property of the poor'.[4] Such pronouncements in his publication *Unto this Last* (1862) represented what was essentially a comprehensive critique of an industrial capitalist system and the policy of free trade which had moral and financial consequences for both the rich and poor.

Ruskin's belief in the honour and value of the individual worker had first been expressed in 'The Nature of Gothic' (1853) when he presented an idealised concept of the medieval craftsman. This essay was to have an inspirational effect on many, including William Morris and Edward Burne-Jones as well as later Lakeland residents and fellow Oxford University students W. G. Collingwood and Hardwicke Rawnsley. It is perhaps easy to understand the attraction of such an anti-mass-industrial message in the rapidly changing and potentially alienating world where, as E. P. Thompson observed, 'young men of the middle classes whose aspirations for a life with finer ends than the amassing of wealth and social position had not been utterly crushed ...'.[5] The romantic appeal of the Middle Ages, when crusaders were assumed to have been inspired by moral causes, was to play a part in the Arts and Crafts Movement and in the paintings of the Pre-Raphaelite Brotherhood. It was also echoed in the somewhat feudal ideals of Ruskin's Guild of St George, which in some ways followed the path set by Feargus O'Connor and his Chartist Land Company launched in 1845. However, where both related to ownership of land, O'Connor had advocated a more widespread radical solution than Ruskin's somewhat idealistic and prescriptive view for community living. In 1871 Ruskin had written

> We will try to make some small piece of English ground, beautiful, peaceful, and fruitful. We will have no steam-engines upon it, and no railroads; we will have no untended or unthought of creatures on it; none wretched, but the sick; none idle, but the dead. We will have no liberty upon it; but instant obedience to known law, and appointed persons: no equality upon it; but recognition of every betterness that we can find, and reprobation of every worseness.[6]

Ruskin's reference to 'no equality' confirmed his preference for a paternalistic hierarchy based on a supposedly Biblical premise and required members, in subscribing to The Guild of St George, which became a legally recognised company in 1878, to 'pledge to give a tenth of their possessions to definite public service'.[7] While Ruskin was intent on bringing cultural change to nineteenth century society by informing the individual's sense of moral consciousness and awareness, it was left to William Morris to develop a more radically collectivist social and political solution.[8] Meanwhile money Ruskin contributed to 'St George's Fund', which he had started in 1871, was allocated for the purchase and protection of land. Diversely, some of the Fund was also used for other projects deemed to improve the environment, one such symbolic gesture included paying the wages of three sweepers to improve the state of London streets. In the Isle of Man and the Lake District funds were used to financially endorse Ruskin's support of rural and craft enterprises, as in the case of the Langdale Linen Industry, and then later in support given to Marion Twelves in Crosthwaite for what became known as The Ruskin Linen Industry.

Marion Twelves, like many participants in the Arts and Crafts Movement, was to make particular reference to the influence of *Fors Clavigera* (as seen in Chapter Four). This volume of work which Ruskin addressed 'to the labourers of England' was intended to relate to some future unstated time 'when we shall have men resolute to do good work, and capable of reading and thinking while they rest ...'.[9] As the introduction in his *Collected Works* was to summarize;

> The only sound condition of society was, he held, one in which every man worked for his living; and of all forms of work, the healthiest and most certainly useful was work upon the land ...[10]

The complexities and contradictions of Ruskin's written work have been given more attention than can be attempted here but it is worth remembering that much of Ruskin's work was more accessible than the weighty library tomes might suggest today. His words were heard not only in public lectures but also, as was the case for *Fors Clavigera*, (1871–1884) through monthly serial publication. *Unto this Last*, credited with influencing the socialist ideals of William Morris, Proust, Tolstoy and Ghandi as well as the first twenty nine Labour M.P.'s elected in 1906, was initially submitted in essay form to the newly created *Cornhill Magazine*. The adverse response to Ruskin's contribution to this publication, however, highlighted the controversial nature of his thinking and the editor William Thackeray felt obliged to curtail their publication in his magazine. Undeterred Ruskin was in the fortunate position of affording to publish his own work and was reassured by his mentor Thomas Carlyle who wrote; 'I have read your paper with exhilaration ... such a thing flung suddenly into half a million dull British heads ... will do a great deal of good'. [11]

Extracts from *Unto this Last* were also arranged by Thomas Barclay into the more accessible format of a pamphlet, entitled *The Rights of Labour*. For 2*d*. one could read the words of 'a great teacher, whose clear, brilliant, and powerful language, is but the fitting conductor of original and valuable thought'. As Ruskin himself stated, within these sixteen pages was 'The best abstract of all the most important pieces of my teaching that has yet been done'. [12]

By the time Ruskin had taken up residence in the Lake District a prodigious number of published works had secured his reputation as one of the somewhat monumental figures of the Victorian Age who, alongside such friends as Charles Darwin, would be deemed a 'quintessential high Victorian intellectual'. [13] It would be, however, a combination of his early writings, when he had attempted to break down aesthetic boundaries in order to value individual craft work, alongside his promotion of rural industries, that would prove to be of particular local relevance. Before outlining some of the social and economic factors which would make the Lake District a favourable place for the practice and marketing of traditional crafts I want to explore the development of what became known as the Arts and Craft Movement through the key figure of William Morris who, as a practitioner, provided a working inspiration to so many.

The working and social ethos of the Arts and Crafts Movement

Mention of William Morris has already been made in terms of John Ruskin's influence on his social and political ideas and there is no doubt that Morris played a crucial role as a practitioner in developing the links Ruskin made between art and society. As David Gerrard succinctly summarised; 'where Ruskin sees his way into a moral world, Morris works his way into it; the first was in all senses a seer, the second a doer'.[14] Following his graduation from Oxford, Morris like Ruskin had considered taking Holy Orders but instead joined the architectural practice of G. E. Street, who by the 1850s had gained a reputation as a leading exponent of the Gothic Revival. Although Morris was to spend only nine months under his tuition, his influence was far-reaching. Street believed architecture was a focal point, 'around which the other arts – painting, sculpture, stained glass, metalwork, and so-on were grouped'.[15] He promoted the use of wall-paintings and stained glass in his buildings and was also familiar with the techniques of embroidery and metalwork. Street's emphasis on the importance of interior design and decoration coupled with Ruskin's elevation of the role of art and craft work legitimised such work to someone of Morris's middle class background.

The subsequent formation of the firm of Morris, Marshall, Faulkner and Co. in 1861 has been well documented and endorsed Ruskin's mandate in *The Two Paths* (1859) in its desire to lead and educate societal taste rather than exploit a market to gain wealth. Morris epitomised this in the now well-known phrase; 'Have nothing in your houses that you do not know to be useful, or believe to be beautiful'.[16] By 1881 the Firm had evolved to become Morris & Co. and moved to larger premises at Merton Abbey where, as others also hoped to emulate,

> Morris envisioned the factory as the centre of a vital community combining production, education, and relaxation with richly functional architecture in harmony with the natural surrounding.[17]

Here he was observed to be a generous and consistent employer not only through paying good wages, despite the fluctuations in trade, but also because of his own thorough knowledge in researching and understanding the working processes of the crafts practised in his workshops.[18] Such high standards and sound employer and worker relationships, however, were not possible without a high end-price. This in turn was to result in accusations of both capitalism and elitism. It was this charge and moral dilemma which would ultimately lead Morris to distance himself from Ruskin's hierarchically ordered teachings and move him to conclude that 'social revolution was the prior condition to the mode of production and consumption necessary to fulfil human nature and bring it into harmony with the environment'.[19]

To accuse Morris of elitism, however, was not totally without foundation. When he was approached to participate in the first exhibition of the newly formed Arts and Crafts Exhibition Society his initial response was somewhat negative. He wrote;

> ... the general public don't care one damn about the arts and crafts; and our customers can come to our shops to look at our goods; and the other kind of exhibits would be some of Walter Crane's works and one or two of Burne-Jones: those would be things worth looking at: the rest would tend to be of amateurish nature, I fear.[20]

His absence from this prospective gathering would have formed a noticeable omission. Since beginning his programme of lectures in 1877 Morris had emerged as a significant influence and leader to many young designers and architects, some of whom had already formed themselves into guilds, echoing the medieval unit for craft workers. These included;

> ... the Century Guild by A. H. Mackmurdo and Selwyn Image in 1882; the Art Workers' Guild in 1884, and the rather more amateur Home Arts and Industries Association in the same year; the Arts and Crafts Exhibition Society in 1886; the Guild of Handicrafts, by C. R. Ashbee, in 1888. The Exhibition Society was founded by a group mainly from the Art Workers' Guild (Benson, Walter Crane, T. J. Cobden-Sanderson, Lewis F. Day, William de Morgan, Lethaby, and Heywood Sumner) who felt that the movement could only make progress through publicity, and that exhibitions were the best form of publicity.[21]

Fortunately, Morris was to relent and participate, so contributing to the exhibition's success when it opened at the New Gallery in Regent Street, London on 4 October 1888. Not only were products from Morris and Co. on display but Morris also delivered a lecture on 'Tapestry'. Later he was to be one of the twenty-two contributors, which included his daughter May, to a collection of informative and wide ranging articles on craft production in *Arts and Crafts Essays* which was published in 1893.[22]

Morris's early concern with standards had been reassured implicitly by the exacting presence of a selection committee. In this way successful exhibitors secured recognition of their individual skills and a visible endorsement of the quality of their craft items, as displayed by the Arts and Crafts Exhibition Society. The fact that all four Lake District industries discussed in this volume exhibited items during the early years of the Society provides evidence of their ability to gain recognition, amongst their peers, on a national platform. It also illustrates the importance of the central role played by the Arts and Crafts Exhibition Society, and other associations, in bringing together participants from around the country and providing a showcase for individual craft-workers.

Concern, however, was to be voiced later in both the 1910 and subsequent exhibitions that the arrangement to exhibit the skills and talents of craft-workers had not been put on a surer footing by securing a permanent central venue. In this way it was felt the artistic capabilities and training practised in groups and workshops 'dotted over the countryside' could be more fully utilised.[23] In perceiving art and craft work to be a national resource Henry Wilson, a leading figure and President of the Society in 1916, criticised the country's failure to endorse or invest in the creative ability that the Arts and Crafts Movement had so clearly brought to fruition. Where some, including Wilson, adhered to the fundamental anti-industrial ideals of the Movement and saw education as the way forward so that every child could participate in craft-work, others prioritised the need for a greater association between craft-workers, designers, manufacturers and retailers. The inevitable split from the, by then, waning Arts and Crafts Exhibition Society occurred resulting in the formation of the Design and Industries Association in 1915. Amongst its founder members was Harold Stabler, whose earlier connections with two of the Lake District industries in Kendal and Keswick had been maintained throughout his developing career. Stabler's first employer, Arthur W. Simpson, was also to be involved with, and lectured to, the Manchester branch of the D.I.A. The Keswick School of Industrial Arts was to benefit from Stabler's later involvement in designing the newly developed stainless steel.[24] To show how the design element of the Movement evolved for some designers and craft-workers, however, is to move away from the social and time-specific perspective of this study where the anti-industrial message confirmed the rural base to be an intrinsic part of the Arts and Crafts Movement. As Fiona MacCarthy summarised:

> Central to this vision was the generous, hopeful theory, especially important in the Arts and Crafts communities, that the labourers of Britain, stunted in the city, would, in a new setting of dignity and harmony, develop their creative instincts to the fullest.[25]

It was for these reasons that Morris, Ashbee and Gill had relocated their urban workshops and workforce to more rural settings, with accompanying mixed results. Alongside these individual craft-based examples, however, were the wider issues of bringing people back to the land in order to counter the effects of industrialisation and the increasing urbanisation of the population.[26]

It is beyond the remit of this discussion to go in to detail about the nineteenth century demographic changes wrought within the context of the industrial revolution. Besides the movement of people, the overall population in England and Wales had doubled within the first half of the century, all of which contributed to a growing concern in the ensuing years about the living conditions and social consequences for those residing in newly formed towns and cities. This situation was compounded further by an agricultural depression during the 1880s forcing more people to seek work in the towns. As an attempt to stem this flow, all party political support was given to the 'Society for Promoting Industrial Villages' to try to revive and consolidate the basis of a rural economy and society. In order to achieve this craft industries were seen to be of particular significance, especially in terms of female employment:

> ... many reformers felt that erratic seasonal work left women in particular underemployed, and thus the reintroduction of craft industries could be seen both as a means towards self-help, part-time work in the home adding to the family's income, and as a way of occupying 'idle hands'.[27]

As a further move to address such issues the Home Arts and Industries Association was founded in 1884 and attracted a predominantly female membership. As the *Artworkers' Quarterly* observed:

> The aim of the Association is to encourage the practice of handicrafts and revive old ones, more especially in villages and country places out of touch with the organisations for art and technical instruction enjoyed by large towns. The classes commence usually by purely voluntary effort on the part of those who have the welfare of country dwellers or working people at heart. Classes are held in the homes of these voluntary teachers, or in rooms lent by others interested in the work. As the pupils become proficient professional teaching is engaged, and perhaps work is executed in response to local orders. The class may in time develop into an industry doing work sufficiently well to attract regular custom, and thus become self-supporting.[28]

Both the Langdale Industry and The Spinnery in Bowness would owe particular allegiance to this association and through the management of Elizabeth Pepper and Annie Garnett regularly exhibited work and gained commissions through the H.A.I.A.'s annual exhibitions, which were held in various venues around the country including the Albert Hall in London. Although, as an earlier citation indicated, it was sometimes regarded as having 'a rather more amateur' approach it nevertheless enjoyed very positive support from a number of Arts and Crafts publications including *The Studio*, which in 1896 felt its influence 'would be considerable, particularly on future generations of craftsmen'.[29] In indicating the broader context within which the ethos of the Arts and Crafts Movement and the Back to the Land Movement influenced the revival of some traditional industries, in this next section I propose to look more closely at the social and economic conditions in the nineteenth century Lake District which inform the background to this study.

A Regional Perspective

While the Lake District owed much to its agrarian economy, to perceive this simply in terms of an idyllic isolated bucolic rolling landscape would be a mistake. The mining of coal, lead, iron, copper and slate together with the production of gunpowder led to the need for a reliable transport network that also benefited the early fell-walkers. The abundance of fast flowing water fed turbines and powered the mill-wheels. The copious forests provided enough wood for manufacturing pencils, baskets, clogs, charcoal and most importantly for much of the nineteenth century, bobbins. With seventy nine bobbin mills in the area, mid-century, the Lake District was able to supply over fifty percent of all requirements for the British textile industry. Bobbin manufacture 'employed hundreds of men and boys, and it made fortunes for not a few solid, hard-driving Cumbrian citizens of yeoman background'.[30] Situated predominantly in the area between Windermere and Kendal the bobbin mills utilised the water-power for wood-turning in this often dangerous and competitive industry which began to decline in the 1870s when faced with cheaper imports from Scandinavia.

Elsewhere mills were grinding corn and water was again utilised at Burneside in the manufacture of paper; initially made from cotton, flax and wool and then after 1874 from straw, jute and imported Norwegian pulp. Wool from the hill sheep was used for making clothing and later carpets. Flax was still grown at the beginning of the nineteenth century in small quantities in the south of Westmorland and used to supply two linen mills at Morland in the production of sailcloth.[31] The continuation of this practice owed something to a tenancy condition for some farms in Cumbria requiring them to grow and process flax into a fabric called 'harden sark'. As Elizabeth Prickett explained, '"Hards" are the coarse fibres of hemp or flax and "sark" was a shirt, though not a shirt as we know it today; it was used as an outer garment'.[32]

Spinning and weaving as a once integral and unifying part of the domestic scene, so celebrated in the Romantic writings of Wordsworth and echoed by Hardwicke Rawnsley, was frequently invoked to contrast with the now more generally perceived fragmented industrial family. Nostalgically this had been a time when:

> The old man, however infirm was able to card the wool as he sat in a corner by the fireside ... Two wheels were often at work on the same floor; and others of the family – chiefly little children – were occupied in teasing and cleaning the wool to fit it for the hands of the carder. So that all except the smallest infants were contributing to the mutual support.[33]

A more pragmatic view, however, was outlined in a later survey as to why this tradition lasted longer in this area than elsewhere.

> Probably the isolated situation of the farms in this mountainous country and the abundance of wool, added to the fact that the stormy weather of the long winter creates a need for indoor occupation, all help to account for the survival here of handspinning and weaving when it had died out in other parts of the country.[34]

Westmorland and the upland areas of Cumberland were indeed some of the most sparsely populated areas in England, but within this were pockets of industrial activity exploiting the natural resources which lay below the surface. These produced, as already mentioned, various minerals and metals including silver, as well as stone and slate to supply the late nineteenth century building programme to the south and west of the region and in the new towns and cities of northern England. In the Langdales, Barbara Russell described '... Elterwater and its neighbour Chapel Stile, both little villages built of the "waste" of the neighbouring slate quarries, contain the larger number of the seven hundred inhabitants'.[35] Those resilient enough to survive such tough conditions often produced large families and although many left the area, the population of Cumberland continued to grow steadily while in Westmorland there was a slight decline between 1881 – 1911. In Cumberland the largest number of migrants were males moving predominantly to Northumberland and Durham while in Westmorland it was mainly women who left in the second half of the century to find work, chiefly in Lancashire and Yorkshire.[36] Coming from an area, which according to the 1851 and 1871 census reports enjoyed a high ratio of school teachers it is perhaps not surprising, as Marshall and Walton observed, that migrants from this area were likely to be amongst the most literate in the country. By 1890 'little Westmorland had overtaken even the metropolis in reducing its ostensible illiterates almost to vanishing point'.[37] The very nature of the regional terrain meant that the majority of the population was concentrated within a comparatively small percentage of the area. A fact which was compounded towards the end of the century with the increasing industrial development of towns like Barrow and Workington. Despite this, agriculture, which included subsidiary trades like quarrying and timber-work, continued to be the single most important industry employing the largest section of the working population during the nineteenth century. The other significant sector was domestic service where approximately a third of the working population found work and whereas these numbers began to fall in Cumberland as the century came to an end, in Westmorland the development of tourism and large residential homes sustained employment in this area.

The main tourist centres in the Lake District at the beginning of the nineteenth century were Bowness and Ambleside on Lake Windermere and Keswick on Derwentwater. Unlike other developing seaside and spa centres, this area drew the visitor who was less interested in the pursuit of physical health but more in 'the intellectual, moral and spiritual benefits derived from the contemplation of lake and mountain scenery', which had so inspired the Lake Poets.[38] Consequently all three towns experienced a substantial increase in the number of residents as well as a concentration of visitors during July and August. Although most stayed in the large hotels, a growing number of Keswick landladies benefited from this seasonal boost to the local economy in the first half of the century. The opening of the Lancaster to Carlisle Railway in 1846 and then subsequently the branch to Windermere in 1847 was to adversely affect the growth of the Keswick tourist trade, before their own line was opened in 1864.

The importance of the railways is highlighted when contrasting figures for a three year period. These revealed that the number of passengers travelling on the Kendal and Windermere Railway was ten times the number of road travellers, who had paid a toll at the Kendal to Windermere turnpike at Plumgarths in 1843–4. Whitsuntide was marked as 'the peak of excursionist activity'.[39] Consequently the Windermere and Bowness area experienced unprecedented growth to accommodate not only the day visitors but more importantly the summer residents, the commuters and those who now chose to spend their retirement in retreat from the industrial towns and cities. The accompanying building programme brought work for many and meant a demand for building materials that not only required more quarrying for local stone and slate but also the dredging of Windermere for sand. This, with the subsequent building on new and infill sites, made a significant change to what had once been an essentially agricultural landscape. The housing development schemes were frequently spearheaded through the entrepreneurial efforts of local people, most notably the Pattinson family. The land they acquired was utilised for building and 'for a while in the 1880s Pattinsons were completing at a rate of one house per day in the Heathwaite area [south east of Windermere]'. The Pattinsons were also responsible for many of the new private roads as well as the hydro-electric scheme at Ghyll Head built to serve the Storrs Estate which they acquired in 1896.[40]

In the 1890s the Pattinson firm was also involved, through their association with the designer and architect C. F. A. Voysey, in building two of the most distinguished houses of the Arts and Crafts Movement period in the area. These were to include Broad Leys, for the Leeds colliery owner and one time mayor of the city Arthur Currer Briggs, and Moor Crag for the textile manufacturers, Buckleys. The presence of such wealthy patrons brought work to both national and local craft-workers and garden designers, including Thomas Mawson. Born locally, Mawson was to establish a national reputation confirmed by his publication of *The Art and Craft of Garden Making* in 1900. He was later to team up with the architect Dan Gibson, who had first come to the area to work on Graythwaite Hall for the Sandys family. Together they undertook a number of design commissions for new houses and gardens including one for the Gaddam family at Brockhole. Other commissions reflected the increased demand for ecclesiastical decoration and Dan Gibson was to collaborate with Arthur W. Simpson, in designing and producing chancel and rood screens for a number of churches including those at Natland, Bowness and Staveley. St James' church at Staveley also

A family photograph of a sitting room at Broad Leys, the house designed by C. F. A. Voysey in 1898. The wallpaper, also by Voysey, provided the setting for the Currer Briggs' own collection of metal and needle work of the Arts and Crafts Movement period. Reproduced by kind permission of Elizabeth Buchanan and with thanks to Wendy & Barrie Armstrong.

contains an impressive stained glass window designed by Edward Burne Jones and made at the Morris and Co. workshops. It forms one local example, amongst many, of significant commissions undertaken within the aesthetic influence of the Arts and Crafts Movement by firms of international repute.[41]

Thomas Mawson also worked on the plans for landscaping the garden at Blackwell, the house designed by Hugh Baillie Scott for the Manchester Brewery owner and Christie's Hospital benefactor, Edward Holt. Holt, like Currer Briggs, held an elevated position within local government and 'enjoyed the very rare honour of being elected Lord Mayor of the city [of Manchester] for two years in a row, in 1908 and 1909'.[42] He was to be a long serving member of the Council's Waterworks Committee, safeguarding his interests as the owner of a brewery. His presence in the Lake District is perhaps not surprising considering that, since the opening of the Thirlmere Reservoir in 1894, Manchester had relied on this natural resource for most of its water supply. It was during this year that the Holts visited Arthur Simpson's establishment at Gill Head. It may be churlish but, as his 1928 obituary concurred, Holt's reasons for acquiring a residence in the area were undoubtedly motivated by his desire to monitor developments at Thirlmere. His concern led him to recommend the acquisition of the Haweswater Estate and subsequently increase the size of the lake and, through some seventy-four miles of piping, link it to the Heaton Park reservoir. It was for this work that Edward Holt was made a baronet in 1916 but he died before the scheme was fully completed.[43]

Holt's presence represents one example of the double-edged benefits brought to the local economy by the presence of a substantial number of wealthy incomers. Besides the work brought in the construction of Blackwell he was to be a generous patron to Dan Gibson who designed his son Joseph's memorial for St Margaret's Church at Prestwich, near Manchester, which was implemented by Simpson's firm. However, for Holt conflict over the utilisation of the landscape was never far below the surface as reflected in an exchange of letters in the *Manchester Guardian.* Local concern was expressed over the replacement of oak trees, whose leaves were deemed to contaminate the water in the Lake at Thirlmere, with the ubiquitous conifers. Re-opening the scars of the beleaguered Thirlmere Defence Association, the charge Alderman Holt sought to answer this time was one of 'destroying the beauty of the woodland ...'.[44] Since the Association's failure to stop the damming of the lake, conservative opposition had regrouped in 1883 in the form of the Lake District Defence Society, led by a committee which included both Hardwicke Rawnsley and Albert Fleming. They at least were amongst the ten percent of the six hundred members who could claim residence in Cumbria and both men have a direct connection with this study.[45]

The challenge of preserving the natural beauty of the Lake District for the enjoyment of residents and visitors, while attending to the cultural heritage and survival of an indigenous population, has echoed throughout the last two centuries. It is within this context that the appeal of an Arts and Crafts Movement, which in its architecture represented a return to the vernacular and within its internal decoration celebrated the individual skill of the craft-worker, was so readily accepted in this area. The presence of the new industrial elite was made more palatable when they were perceived to endorse traditional skills and where architects and designers aimed to blend these new residences into their rural settings. More audacious displays of wealth, however, could still be seen in the yachts and social gatherings on Lake Windermere centred around the Royal Yacht Club.

A greater degree of finesse was also attributed to the visiting tourists, more discerning than those to the nearby seaside resorts of Blackpool and Morecambe, and described as;

> drawn largely from the educated class of high status which could be expected to provide most of its own entertainment ... The visitors occupied themselves entirely out-doors. Sightseeing and contemplation; excursions on foot, by steamer or by road, using the hoteliers' stage-coaches and later the bicycle before motor-cars and charabancs appeared in the early-twentieth century; rowing and fishing on the lake, watching regattas and the occasional tournament; this was the staple fare of the middle-class visitor.[46]

Should it rain, referring to their guide books, visitors could acquaint themselves with one of the local arts and crafts industries. In Keswick, the School of Industrial Arts would undertake commissions for metal and woodwork as well as have some articles of ready-made ornamentation and handicraft on sale. The cottage at Elterwater, set against the impressive Langdale Pikes, could be easily reached from Ambleside or Coniston. Here a variety of pin cushions, lace and domestic items made from Langdale linen could be purchased or orders placed for larger articles while watching a demonstration of spinning and weaving. In Windermere, close to the station, Arthur W. Simpson opened his shop, 'The Handicrafts', as a showroom for the carvings and furniture made at his workshop in Kendal. His wife and son also sold embroideries and had a variety of textiles and fabrics on display. In Bowness, before the New Spinnery opened in 1912, you had to climb the hill by the school to see what the 'Windermere Industries' made at The Spinnery but here, as Baddeley's 1902 guide book stated, were 'things made by hand, particularly Hand-Spun and woven materials, the Teaching of Spinning and Embroidery to village women, and the encouragement of all Art-Work'. More discreetly in the footnote it revealed 'At the Annual Home Arts & Industries Exhibition in London, Windermere [Industries] has recently won the Gold Cross for Design; and has received special distinction for the silk "throwans". At the Albert Hall Exhibition 1898, Windermere obtained 84 awards'.[47]

The Four Lake District Industries

I am aware that concentrating this study on the Langdale Linen Industry, the Simpson Firm of Woodcarvers and Furniture-makers, The Keswick School of Industrial Arts and The Spinnery at Bowness might suggest an absence of any other local craft work. This was clearly not the case. This selection, while owing something to personal interest, was informed by research which revealed the ideological and aesthetic influence of this Movement on the significant individuals involved. On a more pragmatic basis, however, there remains the very real limitations incurred by the availability of relevant archives. I would, for example, if fully documenting those involved in textile work, want to include the Cockermouth firm of Harrison's whose comprehensive array of linen and silk samples are housed at the Victoria & Albert Museum. Their allegiance with the ethos of producing high quality textiles using traditional methods seems unquestionable but in the absence of a documented archive their story remains untold.

The need to maintain a particular focus around the turn of the century when the Arts and Crafts Movement was most active has meant that individuals like Anne MacBeth must also be omitted, albeit reluctantly. Her retirement from the Glasgow School of Art in 1928 resulted in her permanent residence in Patterdale where, with her friend May Spence, she had already established a branch of the Women's Institute in 1921. Encouraging and inspiring local people seemed to form a natural extension to Ann MacBeth's professional working life. In 1900, following her training with Jessie Newberry, she had joined the teaching staff at the school making her an important participant in what became known as the Glasgow Style, described as 'more conventionalised in style than most Arts and Crafts designs, and purer in form than Art Nouveau'.[48] Although frequently overshadowed by Charles Rennie Mackintosh and Margaret and Frances MacDonald, Ann MacBeth proved to be one of the School's most successful teachers and practitioners of embroidery. Like many creative people her retirement from professional employment did not mark the end of her working life. She continued to encourage and inspire local people with embroidery, pottery and ideas for using surplus wool from the indigenous Herdwick sheep. She was to develop her own inventive loom and publish a book entitled *Needleweaving*, in 1926, in collaboration with the Simpson firm in Kendal. This enthusiastic and energetic woman was to leave a lasting memory on many in the area where she was clearly identifiable 'in her flowing cape, her skirt possibly vivid scarlet and emerald green, wearing long necklaces, her small dog Jove by her side'.[49]

Her friendship and working allegiance with Arthur Simpson and his family does serve, however, to underline the significance of his presence within what is generally perceived to be a middle-class Movement. His credentials as a craftsman were unquestionable but his role and connections were clearly enhanced by his teaching and wider commitment to the notion of a 'Simple Life'. For him such an ideology owed much to his Quaker background but it was also a theme closely associated with the Arts and Crafts Movement. Although, as revealed in chapter two, he was clearly committed from a young age to finding a career where he could work with wood, his timing and locality were indeed to prove auspicious. From his Kendal base he was to work with some of the most significant contributors to the Movement and leave the lasting legacy of his craftsmanship in local churches and houses. His craft-base, however, marks a different starting place from the three other founders discussed here. Albert Fleming may have been keen, as shown in chapter three, to call himself a spinner at Langdale but he also practised law in London. Fleming's motives for starting the Langdale Linen Industry owed much to the ideologies of John Ruskin, which he openly acknowledged. This industry, however, was also indebted to the practical assistance of his co-founder Marion Twelves and then later Elizabeth Pepper for its day-to-day running and development. Similarly, Canon Rawnsley as a clergyman and self-appointed protector of the Lake District was motivated by his own social programme, which had been influenced by his early contact with Ruskin at Oxford. This was to include finding practical work for unemployed men and women in his parish as well as providing evening classes to ward off the evil temptation of drink. The Keswick School of Industrial Arts, as seen in chapter four, owed much to Mrs Rawnsley's early artistic and teaching abilities and progressed under the management of appointed skilled craft-workers and designers. Annie Garnett, one of the founders of the Windermere Industries at the Spinnery in Bowness, discussed in chapter five, was similarly inspired by the idea of resurrecting an old craft to provide work in rural areas but went on to develop her role so that, like William Morris, she became an active participant and ultimately a successful textile artist.

This then is the story of four industries whose similarities and differences reflect the diversity of the artistic qualities, technical abilities and ideological beliefs that informed and are included within what is recognised, if not so easily defined, as a significant social and aesthetic Movement. In this regional study of the Lake District I also accept that its somewhat nebulous boundaries may owe more to the words and pictures of artists, poets and guide books than they do to any cartographer and therefore may add to the romancing of this account. Finally, while acknowledging the transient nature of historical knowledge, it has nevertheless been my endeavour to lay down the foundations of a study which hopefully will inspire, inform and encourage further research and publications.

Notes

1. Alan Crawford, *By Hammer and Hand* (Birmingham Museums and Art Gallery, 1984), p. 17.
2. Annie Garnett, unpublished diary entry, January 1900. Garnett Archive, Abbot Hall Museum, Kendal.
3. Catherine W. Morley, *John Ruskin Late Work 1870–1890* (Garland Publishing Inc., 1984), p. 10.
4. Cited in James S. Dearden, *John Ruskin, An Illustrated Life* (The Brantwood Trust, 1981), p. 25.
5. E. P. Thompson, *William Morris. Romantic to Revolutionary* (Merlin Press, 1977), p. 25.
6. Dennis Hardy, *Alternative Communities in Nineteenth Century England* (Longman, 1979), p. 79.
7. Ruskin, *Complete Works*, vol. XXX p. xxiv.
8. See Patrick Scott and Pauline Fletcher (eds), *Culture and Education in Victorian England* (Associated University Press, 1990) for more informed discussion.
9. Ruskin, *Complete Works*, vol. XXVII letter 36 dated December 1873, p. 669.
10. Ibid., p. lviii.
11. James S. Dearden, *John Ruskin, An Illustrated Life*, p. 26. See also Clive Wilmer's discussion in his edited edition of John Ruskin, *Unto this Last* (Penguin, 1985), pp. 28–30.
12. Thomas Barclay (arranged), 'The Rights of Labour according to John Ruskin', in W. Reeves, *Popular Pamphlets by Notable Men*, (London-undated).

13. Frank M. Turner, *Contesting Cultural Authority* (Cambridge University Press, 1993), p. 48.
14. David Gerrard, *John Ruskin and William Morris, The Energies of Order and Love* (Nine Elms Press, 1988), p. 11.
15. Charles Harvey and Jon Press, *William Morris. Design and Enterprise in Victorian Britain* (Manchester University Press, 1991), p. 28.
16. Peter Faulkner, *Against the Age: An Introduction to William Morris* (1980), p. 105.
17. Robert Hewison, *New Approaches to Ruskin* (Routledge & Kegan Paul, 1981), p. 183.
18. Harvey and Press, *William Morris. Design and Enterprise in Victorian Britain*, cite contemporary reports from *The Spectator* and the American *Century Magazine* in 1883 which attest to Morris's good working practices, pp. 146–7.
19. R. Hewison, *New Appproaches to Ruskin*, p. 183.
20. Peter Faulkner (Introduction), *Arts and Crafts Essays* (Thoemmes Press, reprint 1996), pp. vii–iii.
21. Ibid., p. vii.
22. Ibid., preface by William Morris.
23. Walter Crane in *The Catalogue of the 9th Exhibition of the Arts and Crafts Society* (Chiswick Press, 1910), p. 14; and Henry Wilson, *The Catalogue of the 11th Exhibition of the Arts and Crafts Society* (Chiswick Press, 1916), p. 19.
24. See Tanya Harrod, 'The Crafts Around 1916' in *The Crafts in Britain in the 20th Century* (Yale University Press, 1999) and chapters 2 and 4 on the work of Harold Stabler with the Simpsons and at Keswick.
25. F. MacCarthy, *Charles Ashbee, The Simple Life* (Lund Humphries, 1981), p. 10.
26. See comprehensive study in Jan Marsh, *Back to the Land* (Quartet Books, 1982).
27. Brian Harrison, 'Philanthropy and the Victorians', *Victorian Studies*, vol. 9 (1966), p. 371.
28. *Artworkers' Quarterly*, vol. 4 (1905), p. 143.
29. A. Callen, *Angel in the Studio* (Astragal Books, 1979), p. 7.
30. J. D. Marshall, 'The bobbin makers' in *Old Lakeland* (David & Charles, 1971), p. 142. See also J. D. Marshall and M. Davies-Shiel, *The Lake District at Work* (David & Charles), and for photographs see John Marsh, *The Lake Counties at Work* (Alan Sutton, 1995).
31. F. Garnett, *Westmorland Agriculture 1800–1900* (Titus Wilson, 1912), p. 21.
32. E. Prickett, *Ruskin Lace and Linen Work* (B. T. Batsford Ltd, 1985), p. 9.
33. H. Rawnsley, *Ruskin and the English Lakes* (James Maclehose, Glasgow, 1902), p. 131.
34. H. Fitzrandolph and M. D. Hay, 'Decorative Crafts and Rural Potteries', *The Rural Industries of England & Wales Part lll* (Clarendon Press, Oxford, 1927), p. 11.
35. B. Russell, 'The Langdale Linen Industry', *Art Journal* (1897), p. 329.

36. See J. D. Marshall and John K. Walton, Chapter Two 'The economy of the region: its changing shape and structure, 1830–1914', in *The Lake Counties from 1830-mid 20th Century* (Manchester University Press, 1981) for further information.
37. J. D. Marshall and John K. Walton, *The Lake Counties from 1830-mid 20th Century*, p. 141.
38. Ibid., p. 178. See Chapter 8 'The tourist trade and the holiday industry' for a more in depth discussion on this development.
39. From figures cited in J. K. Walton, 'The Windermere tourist trade in the age of the railway, 1847–1912, in O. Westall (ed.), *Windermere in the Nineteenth Century* (CNWRS, revised edition 1991), p. 21.
40. Norman Buckley, 'The Growth of the Settlement of Windermere and Bowness ...' (Dip. History/North West Regional Studies, Lancaster University, 1994), pp. 9, 22–29.
41. See Barrie and Wendy Armstrong, 'A Gazetteer of the Arts and Crafts Movement in the North West' forthcoming publication, which will provide a comprehensive guide to examples of work carried out within the area during this period.
42. Christopher Grayling, *Holt's The Story of Joseph Holt* (Joseph Holt PLC, revised edition, 1998), p. 21. I am indebted to John Borran for my copy of this work and also thank Tim Sturgis for information relating to Blackwell.
43. Ibid., p. 23.
44. *Manchester Guardian*, 25 and 27 January. 1911.
45. See Chapter Nine, 'The defence of Lakeland' in Marshall and Walton, *The Lake Counties from 1830-mid 20th Century* (1981) for a much fuller description.
46. J. K. Walton, 'The Windermere tourist trade in the age of the railway, 1847–1912' in O. Westall (ed.), *Windermere in the Nineteenth Century* (CNWRS, 1991), p. 24.
47. M. J. B. Baddeley, *Thorough Guides; English Lakes* (Dulau & Co., 1902), p. xxx.
48. A. Callen, *Angel in the Studio*, p. 123.
49. Marjory Ives, *The Life of Ann MacBeth of Patterdale* (Patterdale W.I. on the occasion of its Diamond Jubilee, 1981), Other local publication by Margaret Higginson *Artist Ann MacBeth Designer Craftswoman, Her contribution to Art & Craft in Cumbria.*

CHAPTER TWO

The Simpson firm of Woodcarvers and Furniture Makers

> Machine-made furniture, however beautiful the design may be, can never possess the charm of character and individuality which the handiwork of skilled craftsman alone can give. More than that, when furniture is designed to meet definite needs and is made to be useful as well as artistic, it will harmonise perfectly with its surroundings, whether it be in a cottage, a house in a town suburb, or a country mansion. This sense of fitness emphasises the intrinsic beauty of design and workmanship.[1]

In this example of the firm's promotional literature, the words of Hubert Simpson underline their allegiance to the Arts and Crafts Movement. Hubert was the second generation of the family firm, based in Kendal, founded by his father Arthur W. Simpson in 1885. However, where other founders of industries discussed in this volume may have been inspired initially by the ideals of the Movement, Arthur W. Simpson was first of all a craftsman. He served his apprenticeship with Gillows in Lancaster, moving on to Leicester, London and Manchester before finally returning to Kendal to establish a business. His skill and craftsmanship in creating high quality woodcarvings and furniture attracted a wide-ranging clientele which earned him the working and personal friendship of such people as W. G. Collingwood and C. F. A. Voysey. It was, however, through his ability as a teacher, in sharing both his knowledge and philosophies as well as encouraging and bringing people together, that he held a pivotal role within the Arts and Crafts Movement in the Lake District.

In this account of the Simpsons of Kendal and their firm 'The Handicrafts' I aim to retell events relating to a business which benefited from the late Victorian housing boom and was accompanied by an upsurge of interest in craft and design. The firm was then sustained beyond the First World War by an increased demand for church and memorial work. It closed some sixty-five years later when, after the Second World War, there was neither the skilled workers nor the market to carry it on. It is a matter of great

Carved oak sign board used at Queen Katherine Buildings and then later at 'The Handicrafts' at Waterside, Kendal.

sadness that in order to protect his father's standard of work against inferior reproduction the majority of drawings and photographs pertaining to the firm were destroyed in the early 1950s by Hubert Simpson.[2] He was not to know that future historians would revisit the experience of the Simpson's, their furniture would sell for four-figure sums in auction houses and the role his father played within his home town of Kendal and the Lakeland hills would be recognised within the broader national context of The Arts and Crafts Movement.

An incomplete public archive means that this account owes much to Eleanor Davidson and her book, *The Simpsons of Kendal – Craftsmen in Wood 1885–1952*, which because of her unique access to family and business records, family members and past employees becomes a primary source, in itself, for the history and work of this family firm. My retelling of the story of the Simpsons does not claim to be fully comprehensive but, within the brevity of this space, to present a social history of the firm within the context of the Arts and Crafts Movement, which by its very nature is inextricably linked with people, their networks and biographical details.

The Founder – Arthur W. Simpson

Arthur was born on 7 December 1857. He was the first child of William and Eleanor Simpson who ran a confectionery shop in Highgate, the main street of South Lakeland's major town, Kendal. The business was not a success and the family moved to Strickland Place from where William Simpson began working for Whitwell, Braithwaite and Nelson of Gandy Mills. Although he had trained as a tailor's cutter he remained in this employment as a salesman and carpet cutter for the next thirty five years until his death in 1892. Arthur's mother, Eleanor, had been a student at the Manchester School of Design but in response to family business and domestic difficulties she had been forced to cut short her attendance. As parents, it was perhaps for these reasons that they remained supportive to their son in his choice of vocation. Arthur in turn paid tribute to his mother's skills from which he was to benefit, writing; 'No artist was ever keener in trying experiments and the number of fresh dishes was simply amazing. Her artistic instinct, that joy of doing things well, manifested itself in her cookery'. [3] Money was to be an on-going concern, as Arthur's later scrap book reveals. He was to collect many cuttings, including one entitled 'How "we two" live on 18*s.* 6½*d.*' dated 1904 which challenged a previous article in its claim of 'How to Live on One Pound per Week'. Other undated articles are headed 'Marriage on £80 a year' and more ambitiously 'Can Two Cultured People live on £100 a year?'. Just how successful Arthur and his wife were to be in this respect is unknown but it aligns him with Edward Carpenter and Charles Ashbee who, like others, were to advocate the merits of a 'Simple Life' and 'the absence of things'.[4] During Arthur's formative years, he had no doubt been influenced by his mother's admirable example. On £1 a week, as he later recalled; 'Five of us were provided with food and washing and cleaning out of this sum, and throve on it. The food was varied, nourishing and plentiful. The house was spotless and well-ordered, the clothes were warm, if plain, and the weekly charwoman, kept for years were all paid out of this £1 per week'.[5]

Despite this conscientious background, Arthur was recorded as a reluctant pupil in his encounter with formal education at the Stramongate Friends' School in Kendal where, under the head-ship of Henry Thompson, only his drawings were deemed noteworthy. His out-of-school activities attracted more attention, though not always of the positive kind. Whittling marvellous creations from wood with his penknife doubtless impressed his friends, though for helping himself to sticks from his father's favourite tree he was to receive repeated thrashings.[6] When he was eleven his parents,

Quakers by background if not practice, sent Arthur away to the Friends' school at Rawden, near Leeds. He returned to Kendal to complete his secondary education at Stramongate before leaving at the age of fourteen in 1871, by the mutual consent of both pupil and his parents. It is somewhat ironic that the reluctant student was one day to be known endearingly as 'the Professor'. Like many who recognise missed educational opportunities and the need for a broader more flexible curriculum, to suit those more at ease with practical tasks, Simpson was to return to his old school, this time in the role of teacher. In this capacity his efforts and diligence, in inspiring pupils in the woodwork workshop, were acknowledged with gratitude at the Stramongate prize day in 1893.[7] Similarly, the ethos of the Quaker teachings was to have a lasting and fundamental effect on Arthur's way of thinking.

Learning the Trade

In Kendal there were few opportunities for apprenticeship in wood-carving, even though Bingham records that there were five cabinet makers on the Trades Register in 1873.[8] In 1872 the young Simpson joined the new cabinet-making business of Robert Rigg, in Greenhow's Yard, as the second apprentice. Here it was hoped that he would learn how to use tools and wood so that his leisure activity could become a somewhat more useful occupation. To begin with all seemed well, he was to recall; 'The first job was making a dovetailed box. How I laboured over that box. What difficulty I felt in squaring up the wood for it, and how, bit by bit, I made myself useful'.[9] Rigg's business was not confined to wood-work but included more general purpose building, painting and decorating. Simpson was not interested in these and was even more appalled by the firm's role as undertakers. When, at the age of fifteen, his employer's absence meant Simpson was expected to lift a body in to a coffin he resolved to find a new position.

Luckily Simpson had not been 'bound' at Rigg's and when he heard of a possible opening for an apprenticeship in carving at Gillow's in Lancaster he wrote and subsequently was interviewed. Samuel James Harris, the head of Gillow's and the foreman carver, James Fairweather agreed to take him on and Simpson joined the firm shortly before his eighteenth birthday on 4 October 1875. Little is known of his workshop experiences but from the long room that overlooked Damside Street he came to appreciate the importance of a good light source to the carver. Much of the work was repetitious, concentrating on the need for accuracy and in this young Simpson found an inspiring role model in his foreman, 'who could execute

The young A. W. Simpson.

foliage panels by the dozen, and whatever he undertook, was well done'.[10] It is perhaps worth reinforcing the point that Arthur W. Simpson trained as a woodcarver with Gillow's and not as a cabinet maker.

While in Lancaster Simpson found lodgings in Castle Street with the turnkey of the castle. Despite describing these as 'joyless', he stayed for the next three years paying 5 shillings a week. The food, however, was of such poor quality that ill-health forced Simpson to forego his vegetarian diet and take up a physical training regime. 'Once or twice a week he would strip off to walk or run a mile or two against the clock. On other days they would have a seven or eight mile walk ...'.[11] In this he was often accompanied, on summer evenings after work, by his bench-mate William Murray who was deaf and dumb and for whom Simpson learnt sign language in order to communicate.

Walking was to be an important element of Simpson's life, not simply in order to get from A to B or in his case, Lancaster to Kendal or even, as in one instance, London to Kendal; but as a social and therapeutic activity that literally broadened his horizons. A scrapbook he kept, gives some indication of the development of his wider interests but also reflects the growing popularity of walking as a leisure pursuit. A number of newspaper cuttings were selected for their practical information on rucksacks, foot-wear, the 'bivouac' cooker, hammocks and sleeping bags as well as reports on various routes, including one for Land's End to John O'Groat's. An undated article by his friend W. G. Collingwood celebrated 'The Revival of Walking' and observed an increase in the number of walkers now to be seen in the Lake District and on the fells. He wrote;

> Lovers of scenery are venturing to assert their opinion, and going to nature in the only way possible to them – by taking their walks abroad.

> It is not only the craze of walking races, nor yet the limited, though influential, ambitions of crag-climbers, that seem to have brought the change about. I hope it is more than that, and anticipate a real revival of the oldest, the noblest, and (which matters a good deal to many of us) the cheapest form of sport.[12]

Two photographs of a party of crag climbers including 'AWS', as well as a booklet from the 'Manchester Pedestrian Club' and a record of several walking itineraries, serve to underline the gregarious side of his pastime.

Other articles reflect even more positive gains including some amazingly restorative claims. One declared 'Walking forces one to forget business worries. One undertakes a walk in order mainly to forget everything …', while another undated and unattributed article states;

> The power for mental work is increased, the view of one's duties and its worries and hardships is corrected, and often I have observed that the hair of the head and beard, when commencing to turn grey, has resumed, after good courses of climbing, more or less of the original colour.

Whether this was the case for the once sandy-haired Simpson is not recorded. The quest for self-improvement and the ability to cover long distances on foot were, however, to prove to be significant factors in Simpson's career.

While in Lancaster he spent the winter evenings attending the nearby School of Art in order to increase his skills as a designer. His ideas about education were clearly changing and his positive enthusiasm was to increase his desire to teach his own craft which, together with his love of walking, would ultimately be to the gain of a number of rural villages in Westmorland.

The completion of his apprenticeship of three years and sixty four days was marked with his twenty-first birthday celebrations, which took place after work, in a pub in St Nicholas Street. It was recorded that while others participated in rum punch Arthur, in keeping with his Quaker beliefs, consumed only ginger beer. More lavish celebrations took place in Kendal the following weekend with the aid of his mother's copious confectionery talents. He was to walk to Kendal with his art school friend Edward S. Bayley and they returned to Lancaster afterwards. Here Arthur continued to work for Gillows for another nine months before starting on a more independent path as a journeyman.

Simpson – the Journeyman

Armed with a prestigious apprenticeship Arthur W. Simpson travelled to Leicester where he was to live with an aunt and uncle, Thomas and Lizzie Seddon. Here he found work with Samuel Barfield, a master carver, who designed work for some thirty carvers under his supervision. It was during this time that Simpson sought to consolidate his affinity with the Quaker ethos and at the age of twenty three he became a member of The Society of Friends.[13] His geographical roots, however, were firmly established in the north west and following a visit home to Kendal, for Christmas 1880, he made his first attempt to set up a workshop there. *The Westmorland Gazette* for 22 January 1881 contained the following brief advertisement; 'Arthur W. Simpson, Architectural and General Wood Carver, 22a Highgate, Kendal'.

The first job carried out in his workshop next to the publisher, stationer and bookseller Titus Wilson, was to carve the capital letters on the regalia of the Masons for the Masonic Hall. Unfortunately, few commissions followed and what he did manage to do made little impact on a debt he accrued to an uncle for £30. While acknowledging his own limited experience Simpson concurred that 'Kendal was not the best place in the world for a carver'. [14] In deciding on his next move he sought the advice of his old foreman from Gillows, James Fairweather, who had been working in Paris. He advised Simpson to move to London where he would be more likely to find a better quality of work and pay. So it was that in early 1882 Simpson, who so loved the countryside, found himself trudging the streets of London but nevertheless determined to succeed in his chosen vocation.

Eventually, he found work with Osmond's, a firm in Finsbury which supplied carvings to cabinet makers and the building trade. He was fortunate in finding digs in Peckham with a family from Kendal who 'sometimes gave me a dinner when I was too poor to spend rashly out of my few shillings'.[15] This bleak time consisted of long hours at the bench after a considerable walk to work, of some four to five miles, along city pavements. After work he frequently spent time in the Architectural Museum in Westminster working on modelling before returning to his digs. During a particularly depressing time it was a visit to the museum at Bethnal Green, where he saw a cabinet designed by a Paris firm and an inspirational book about the wood carver who worked on St Paul's Cathedral, that his enthusiasm for his craft was renewed and he vowed to make another attempt to find a more prestigious workshop. To this end he made a rather special visiting card that was to prove successful. As he recorded;

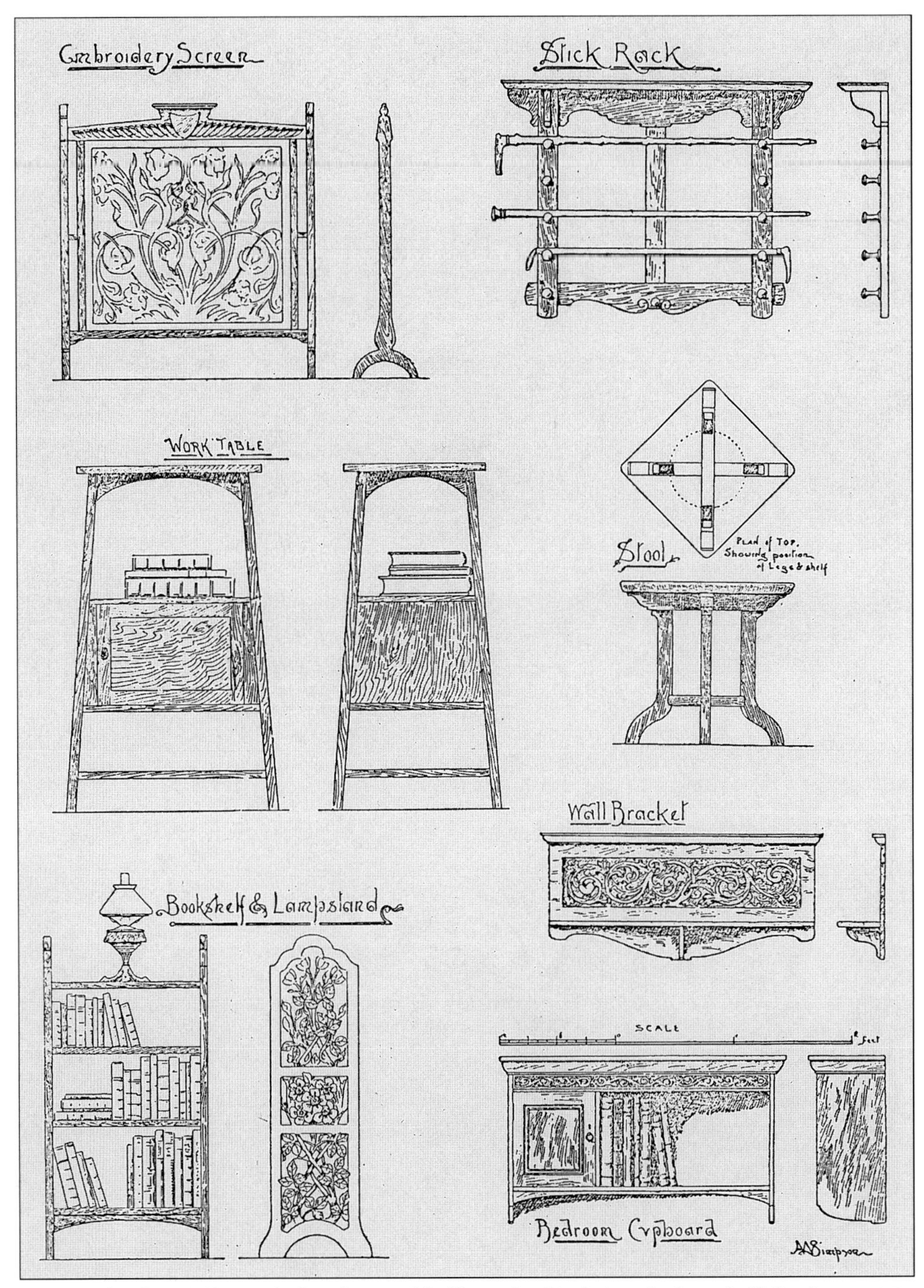

An example of A. W. Simpson's draughtsmanship illustrating his designs for household furniture.

> I got a piece of pear wood and after much trouble with the design, I carved a panel of conventional foliage. How well I remember the shaky dressing table on which I worked – but I believe it was this which got me the job at Aumonier's in Tottenham Court Road.[16]

Simpson described William Aumonier as 'a genial soul who made charcoal drawings for us to work from. He had no packer, no clerk, no handy man and so kept down expenses'.[17] In 1885 Aumonier was elected to The Art Workers' Guild, initially a somewhat exclusive and introspective association of artists, architects and designers keen to unite as a professional body. Simpson, himself was to be elected some twenty eight years later. Unlike The Arts and Crafts Exhibition Society formed in 1888, however, it was not as outgoing in promoting its ideals to the public at large.[18] Unfortunately, despite initially spending long hours at his bench, from 8 until 7, the amount of work Aumonier's generated in 1882 was not enough to sustain Simpson's employment for long. In leaving London and in response to a commitment to attend a family wedding in Kendal, Simpson decided to make the long journey home on foot. This 252-mile walk, with accounts of people that he met on the way and the places that he visited, was to become part of his family legend.

The need to find further work meant his stay at home was short and this time he travelled to the Manchester area and found an opening with Faulkner Armitage, an artist and designer who had working premises in Church Street in Altrincham. Although only eight years his senior, Armitage may have proved to be the successful role model Simpson needed. His Congregationalist and Liberal party activities provided a broad social spectrum and during his three year stay Simpson made the acquaintance of a number of important contacts as well as familiarising himself with his own extended family and local members of The Society of Friends.

Simpson's return to Kendal in 1884 appeared to be prompted by an illness but there are no real details. It is known, however, that in the following July Simpson opened a workshop at 25 Finkle Street. Much of the information relating to this period has been pieced together by Eleanor Davidson with the aid of correspondence from Edward Sutton, a Manchester Friend Simpson had met in his previous position. In the August Sutton helped his friend to draft a promotional circular and wrote that he was 'Very glad to hear that work comes in steadily. I have always been of the opinion that it was a right step to remove to Kendal and I think thou hast every right to be satisfied both as regards improved health and prospects before thee'.[19] Confirmation that this time Simpson viewed his residence as more permanent was made clear by his application to have his Friends' Removal Certificate transferred from the Ashton-on-Mersey Meeting to Kendal later that year. This time he was putting roots down in Kendal for good.

Establishing a reputation and business in Kendal

Soon after his return to Kendal Simpson became involved in teaching a carving class in the small nearby market town of Milnthorpe. A year later a notice in the *Kendal Mercury and Times*, relating events from the Kendal Literary and Scientific Institute, recorded

> ... Mr Simpson gave a practical demonstration in Wood-carving. A handsome hat-rack was exhibited as the work of some of Mr Simpson's pupils at Burneside, some panels from Gatebeck and a beautiful hanging cabinet was contributed by Mr Simpson himself.[20]

In November, later that year, *The Westmorland Gazette* reported on another carving demonstration and lecture that Simpson gave, entitled 'Art at Home', in the schoolroom at Endmoor, so adding another village along with Milnthorpe, Gatebeck and Burneside to his increasing number of teaching venues. In carrying out this work Simpson was putting into practice Ruskin's ideal of promoting traditional crafts in rural areas and sharing in his views on the relevance of good art for all, regardless of wealth and position. Clearly influenced not only by the words of John Ruskin but also those of Edward Carpenter and William Morris, Simpson endorsed the view that 'Simplicity in life, even the barest is not misery, but the very foundation of refinement'.[21]

His scrapbook confirms this with a number of articles, clipped from newspapers and magazines, on domestic budgeting and thrift which suggests his interest was not one necessarily borne out of necessity but complied with the ethos of the Quaker ideology. It was also an inherent part of the Arts and Crafts Movement for some practitioners, in their quest for a 'Simple Life'.[22] One citation from Morris that he chose to keep, was printed in sepia with an embellished first letter and read:

> But look, suppose people lived in little communities among gardens and green fields, so that you could be in the country in five minutes' walk, and had few wants, almost no furniture for instance, and no servants, and studied the (difficult) arts of enjoying life, and finding out what they really wanted: then I think we hope civilization had really begun!

Simplicity and the dislike of excess were central to Simpson's beliefs, as they were to The Society of Friends. It is not surprising therefore to learn how troubled he was before accepting his first church commission for a piece of carving. Besides his own work, which was to be at St Catherine's Church at Crook, he was also involved with supervising a class at Burneside in their carving of the Parish Church reredos. His identity as someone 'of ancient Kentdale Quaker stock'[23] was only reconciled with these commissions after much anxious consideration, as witnessed through his correspondence with his friend Edward Sutton. In later life Simpson justified his reasons, for fulfilling what were to be a large number of ecclesiastical commissions, in a pragmatic way stating; 'I do my work to the greater Glory of God; if in so doing, it helps others to worship God, I am happy to work for churches or institutions, even though I do not share their beliefs'.[24]

Besides teaching, Simpson was also busy with his first exhibition which, as reported in *The Westmorland Gazette* on 12 June 1886, he held at Finkle Street. Alongside his own work were paintings by Mr and Mrs W. G. Collingwood, some of them framed by Simpson. This friendship, which probably began through a mutual connection in Burneside and the carving classes held there, was to be a lifelong association. Letters in the family collection from Collingwood reveal discussions relating to many instances of the two men collaborating on particular projects. Amongst these was the drafting of a programme of nine lectures for the Oxford University Extension Course which was to be held in Coniston in the Spring of 1887. Simpson was to deliver three lectures on wood carving while his fellow tutor spoke on subjects related to minerals. Collingwood would also seem to be the most likely candidate to have introduced Simpson to John Ruskin, whom he saw occasionally at Brantwood.

Simpson's friendship with Collingwood was also fuelled by a mutual enjoyment of walking. Despite his enthusiasm, however, Collingwood declined one invitation from the man only four years his junior not just on the basis of pressure of work but, in attesting to Simpson's fitness, that 'you, energetic man, would walk me off my legs in half a day'.[25] Collingwood was to remain a constant and positive influence to Simpson, supporting and encouraging him to be steadfast in his ideals and business, writing on one occasion: 'We must keep hammering at it. Kendal is a very dark place'.[26]

It is clear, however, that Simpson had broader horizons in mind. In 1889 he visited Paris. Unfortunately there is no record of who accompanied him or whether there was a particular purpose. In the same year, he made his first piece of carving, a panel of dog roses, to be accepted by the Arts and Crafts Exhibition Society for display in London; but they rejected one of his cabinets. In Kendal, he was

The oak casket designed and made by Simpson to contain the parchment conveying the freedom of the borough of Kendal to James Whitehead, Lord Mayor of London. The three panels at the front of the casket replicate the coat of arms for the Corporation of Kendal and that of the Lord Mayor, together with a central panel containing a monogram dated 1889. There were also three intricately carved back panels, together with side panels showing views of Kendal Castle and the Kendal Parish Church.

chosen to make a casket of Danzig oak, which was formally presented to the town's first Freeman. James Whitehead, later Sir James, had started his working life locally as an apprentice draper but went on to greater acclaim and became a Lord Mayor of London. The casket, designed and carved by Simpson drew some criticism from his friend Collingwood, who thought 'the buttresses a little meagre and not quite in keeping with the picturesque panelling'.[27]

Such observations, however, did not preclude his custom and when the Collingwoods moved from Gill Head to their new home at Lanehead, Coniston in 1891 Simpson's firm was asked to make them several items of furniture. These included a semi-circular window seat and a settle with cane seating. The writing table, music stand and corner cupboard made out of ash were, as Collingwood instructed and as was fashionable at the time, all stained green. They clearly met with satisfaction as Collingwood responded idiosyncratically: 'Thank you for carrying out my intentions so nicely. I don't think them open to any criticism ... they are each and all absolutely simple and sensible with the maximum of individuality and unusualness'.[28] The removal of the Collingwood family from Gill Head, as shown later, was to provide Simpson with an opportunity to take his teaching philosophies a step further.

1891 was also the year of Kendal's Arts, Crafts, and Loan Exhibition with a formidable number of exhibits from a wide range of Westmorland industries. Recognition of Simpson's increasing status as a craftsman and businessman was reflected both by his presence on the elected executive committee and by the size of his exhibit in the Drill Hall. The exhibition was given royal patronage and was opened by the Queen's daughter, the Princess Louise. Unfortunately, but perhaps not surprisingly, the proceedings were somewhat dampened by heavy rain. *The Westmorland Gazette*, in giving full coverage to the event, paid this tribute to Simpson's work.

> Another exhibit which attracts by its artistic beauty is that of Mr. Arthur W. Simpson, of Kendal, who has a corner fitted up as a carving studio. The most conspicuous piece of work exhibited by Mr Simpson is a piano screen in light oak, with wings which move backwards and forwards on castors, each wing having a panel of pale green silk, which produces a very delicate effect. The centre panel of the screen bears an appropriate quotation from Longfellow in gold letters, and one or two small brackets and a lower shelf give an appearance of utility to what is really a novel and charming piece of work. A small fireside wall cabinet is another of Mr Simpson's productions. It is made of oak, and carved, and is designed for the reception of an odd book or two, pipes, or a newspaper, and would be delightfully appropriate by a smoking-room fireside, the carved inscription – 'Oh for a Booke and a Shadie Nooke' adding to its air of comfortable quaintness. Mr Simpson also exhibits one or two carved panels and an old-fashioned spinning stool which is very quaint.

Tribute was also paid to his role in providing 'a great impetus in the county and neighbourhood during past few years through classes formed . . .'.[29]

Simpson had clearly made sound progress in the intervening years since his advertisement in *The Westmorland Gazette* on 6 November 1886 had stated:

> Arthur W. Simpson
>
> Designs and Manufactures Furniture on the Premises;
> And also undertakes the entire fitting of houses in
> an Artistic and Economical manner.

Another measure of this success was his move, in 1887, to more spacious premises in Berry's Yard, not far from his Finkle Street room. In May of that year an exhibition was held there which included not only the work of the Collingwoods but also other local artists, amongst them Arthur Severn and Hubert Coutts. Also represented were exhibits from the Keswick School of Industrial Arts and a spinner demonstrating her craft on a wheel. Local newspaper reports again paid tribute to the quality of the exhibits and the work by his students noting; '... they mark the astonishing progress that has been made under Mr Simpson's teaching ...'.[30] His enthusiasm for teaching classes as far afield as Lancaster, Hawkshead, Sedbergh, Bolton-le-Sands, Burneside and Gatebeck, again reflected his stamina and his love of walking.[31] By this time he was not only an acclaimed teacher but also an employer.

Employees

While no clear records exist for this early period, his first employee was Tom Dixon, a neighbour from Finkle Street, who joined the firm on 9 April, 1886. Not yet twenty-one and never having served an apprenticeship, he went on to become a fine craftsman and wood turner in the days before the electric lathe. He was to be the longest serving employee and remained with the firm until his death in 1930. He was also a gifted instrument maker, producing violins and 'cellos from a workshop in his own house. A more experienced craftsman, William Philipson, was taken on to fulfil the role of foreman cabinet maker. It was he who supervised the production of the Simpson furniture and who was responsible for training and frightening a number of apprentices; just how many boys actually came and went from the benches at this time is not known. William Mathews, another cabinet maker, also joined the firm around this time and left in 1893 to set up his own business in Stramongate in Kendal.

The first known pupil or apprentice carver Simpson took on was Harold Stabler, son of the school master at Levens. He stayed with the firm until he became a full-time teacher at the Keswick School of Industrial Arts in 1898, where he stayed for two years before moving on to greater national acclaim.[32] Whilst in Kendal, Stabler gained an Art Teacher's Certificate and won many prizes for his designs at the Kendal Art and Technical School. In 1893 he was joined by fellow apprentice carver Esmond Rigby, son of Cuthbert Rigby who was a Lakeland artist and friend of Simpson. Rigby provided some of the drawings for the firm's circulars and letter headings. Also employed at this time were Ben Dawson, William Newby, Jack Robinson and Richard Bindloss and Miss Tanner, the first clerk. Besides the concerns of running a business, book-keeping, placating difficult customers, maintaining standards and finding new customers, Arthur W. Simpson was gaining other new and personal responsibilities.

Family Man

In 1887, at the age of thirty, Simpson became engaged to Jane Davidson, a qualified nurse who worked at the Kendal Memorial Hospital. They married in the following March at the Friends' Meeting House at Preston Patrick, near Milnthorpe, and made their first home in a small house in Gandy Street, Kendal. Although previously uninvolved with craft work Jane proved to be competent at embroidery and leatherwork, going on to display her work at the exhibitions in Coniston. Inspired by May Spence and the multi-talented Ann MacBeth, who were both customers and family friends, Jane also decorated pottery which was fired in the kiln Spence and MacBeth had set up in Patterdale. Jane's sewing skills and knowledge were to add another dimension to the business, which became most evident when later the Simpsons opened a shop in Windermere.

In the year after their marriage Hubert was born, followed by Ronald in 1890 and Hilda in 1892. Not surprisingly this development brought about a change of address to Broom Close Cottage on the Sedbergh Road (near to where, some twenty years later, Littleholme was built) and then to number 4, Town View. As Eleanor Davidson

The Simpson family at Gill Head; Arthur, Hilda, Jane, Ronald and Hubert.

noted of the latter, 'Situated as it was, almost directly opposite the Workhouse and at the bottom of the House of Correction Hill, the Simpson children were brought up aware of the need for social work. They learnt very young to play with the work-house children and a visit to "The Slums" is mentioned in Hubert's first diary'.[33]

During this time Simpson maintained his teaching commitments, many of which were undertaken after a day's work. His friend, Edward Sutton, counselled 'this has always seemed to me a laborious part of thy occupation. I do not know what remuneration it brings – but unless it distinctly gets thee more profitable work, it is hardly worth continuing. We all consider it very laborious to go so far and return home so late'.[34] This seems particularly true of one teaching venue at Sedbergh. By the time the class had finished it was too late to catch the last train so Simpson had to walk the ten miles home. Family memories recall that on dark winter evenings his wife Jane would walk up on to the fell road to meet him. His motive for running these classes clearly went beyond any notion of financial remuneration. It would seem his reward was the enthusiasm and confidence gained by his students through their enjoyment and satisfaction of making and designing things. In a broader context it clearly identifies Simpson's commitment to the growth of art and craft classes in village schools which Ruskin was so keen to encourage, nationally and locally. It also reflects the growing influence of the Home Art and Industries Association and later the Rural Industries Co-operation Society where professional teachers were engaged to promote traditional crafts and so provide work for people in the countryside.[35] Closer to home, in Kendal, Simpson was also teaching wood carving to over seventy students in three different classes in 1892. Eventually this would become part of the curriculum provided by The Kendal School of Art and Science. With confidence in the success of his teaching and the business now more established at Berry's Yard, Simpson embarked on another venture. Taking on the tenancy of the cottages at Gill Head, one-time home to the Collingwoods, he opened a summer school. As Hardwicke Rawnsley described;

> At Gill Head, Arthur Simpson, a true follower of Ruskin's teaching, and one who is proud of his profession as a maker and designer of furniture for household purposes, has been able to open a summer school and to help a good number of willing pupils each year to learn something of the secrets of wood-craft in such scenery as keeps the heart at peace and the eyes filled with the reverence of nature.[36]

Gill Head

Plans for such a scheme had been developing since Easter 1883, with the help of Manchester and Cheshire friends who often joined the Simpsons at a cottage the family rented for week-ends and holidays at Stang End, which lies not far from Elterwater between Little Langdale and Little Fell. Besides the excursions of climbing and walking in the hills, discussions were held regarding the possibilities of opening a residential school of carving. By Whitsun Simpson had secured the tenancy for Gill Head, sent out the circulars, furnished the cottage, put up his sign and moved the family in.

Originally three cottages that were roughly knocked into one, Gill Head had remained empty on the side of the road between Bowness and Newby Bridge since the Collingwoods' departure. Simpson was now able to rent it for a small sum of money. His son, Hubert, recalled that inside they had inherited a lively and interesting legacy, thanks to the talents of the previous occupants.

> There were several painted doors – the most striking being in the dining room – a design of oriental poppies decorating a brown batten door, otherwise untouched from the saw. Two bedroom doors had daisies painted on them and there was a well under the side-board in the dining room.

The letter-heading for the school at Gill Head, drawn by Cuthbert Rigby.

In the middle of the sitting room there was a wooden post supporting the ceiling, 'on which notches were cut to record each child's height …'.[37] It was above this room that Simpson created a studio to teach his pupil carvers.

For eight years the family of five, together with two young servants, would move into Gill Head at Easter where they would spend the summer before leaving in September. Simpson would commute to his business in Kendal for three days of the week and spend the rest of his time at Gill Head. If and when he was unavailable then Harold Stabler fulfilled the teaching role.

The first pupils to arrive were the Hunt sisters from Shrewsbury, possibly responding to an advertisement which had been placed in the prospectus of the National Home Reading Union or one of the circulars sent to existing customers. They, like their successors, enjoyed the combination of specialist tuition and dramatic rural surroundings. Some of the guests stayed with the family while others found accommodation in nearby hotels and houses. The cottage, near Lake Windermere and surrounded by woods, did indeed prove to be a joyous setting for learning a new skill, as seen by the many entries in the visitors' book. One entry, made on 19 August 1893, in Simpson's own strong handwriting recorded some of the more energetic adventures.

> No resident pupils today – so took the steamboat to Waterhead and there met Miss Forte, and with my wife and daughter, Hilda, (aged 9 months and one day) took the chara-banc to Grasmere and from there climbed Helvellyn (3118 feet high), then down Wythburn, and on by road to Grasmere. My wife carried Hilda most of the way and none of the party much tired. There was a fine breeze, with occasional heavy showers, and the cloud effects, and scenery were magnificent. 6½ hours including stoppages. Arthur Simpson.[38]

Many of the pupil carvers who did attend were women, reflecting the acceptability of this activity, as Anthea Callen described, as a suitable pastime and occupation for young women.[39] None, however, could have found such a public place for their work as May Spence, who was to spend two weeks at Gill Head in 1897. Her father was the harbour master at North Shields and later she was to carve a new 'dolly' to be placed on the quay, replacing the old one worn by the superstitious seamen who would not set sail before touching it.

Besides pupils, fellow craftsman and others involved in teaching also visited the summer school. These included Richard Rathbone from Liverpool, J. R. Jolly from the Preston School of Art, William Ripper from Sheffield and B. I. Fletcher from the Leicester School of Art. From the Keswick School of Industrial Arts, Canon and Mrs

Rawnsley called on numerous occasions. Having established their school in its permanent premises in 1894, they were to engage Simpson to teach there for the winter session in 1896 for 27/6*d.* per lesson. This commitment was again shared with Harold Stabler who taught on alternate Tuesdays. Later Stabler was to join the staff at Keswick on a more permanent basis, as their Head of the School in 1898.[40] On 11 August 1900, besides 'Members & friends of the Friends Quarterly Meeting Cycle Club' and others calling at Gill Head, Annie Garnett from the Spinnery in Bowness, her sister Frances, Mrs Willingham Rawnsley,[41] W. G. Groves of Holehird, Mrs Charles Brand of New York City and Edward and Elizabeth Holt of Blackwell all signed the Visitors' Book.

The Holts had first visited Gill Head in 1894, the same year in which Sir John James Harwood, the Chairman of the Waterworks Committee for Manchester, had opened the Thirlmere Reservoir. Holt a fellow committee member, who later became Lord Mayor of Manchester from 1907 to 1909, was to be an important patron to Simpson, employing him and his firm to work on Blackwell, the house designed by Baillie Scott. Holt also commissioned a significant number of carvings for St Margaret's Church in Prestwich including the choir stalls, which were designed by the Windermere based architect Dan Gibson. Edward Holt was a successful brewer who like fellow industrialist Currer Briggs and other commercial entrepreneurs commissioned the building of prestigious holiday homes in the Lake District. Holt's house at Blackwell was sited close to Gill Head and this may have been yet further reason to ask Simpson to work on the wood panelling, the staircase and the decorative screen that hid the small smoking room, above the fireplace, from the hall below. Although Blackwell was completed in around 1900 Simpson's firm continued to work on the inside of the house throughout the 1920s.[42] Besides Baillie Scott and Dan Gibson, Simpson was to work with the renowned architect and designer C. F. A. Voysey, who was commissioned and built two other significant Lakeland houses of The Arts and Crafts Movement era: Broad Leys for the Leeds colliery owner Currer Briggs and Moor Crag for the textile manufacturers, Buckleys.

Although there is no record of their first meeting, a chair exhibited in the Arts and Crafts Exhibition Society in 1896 was designed by Voysey and executed by Simpson. As Voysey's most recent biographer, Wendy Hitchmough, stated: 'One of the furniture-makers who Voysey occasionally used, and whose affinity for the inherent beauty of wood may well have influenced his designs, was Arthur W. Simpson'. At Broad Leys, Voysey specified that Simpson was to make the balusters, which were inlaid with lead hearts, as well as a deal seat for the veranda.[43] Later, as shown, when Simpson needed plans for the building of his own house, Littleholme, he entrusted the work to his friend Voysey.

Gill Head was not only successful as a school and for the many business contacts it attracted but it also proved to be a most congenial place for social activities and enjoyment. As Maggie Dawson was to record in the Visitors' Book on July 1st 1893; 'Three of the happiest weeks I will spend. Surrounding outside, most congenial. Success to the Gillhead [sic] venture'. A year later on Whit-Sunday, Arthur Piggot, one of those present at the initial Easter discussions, showed that he was not only a supportive customer of the Simpson firm but also something of a poet. Waxing lyrical in prose, before launching into verse, he wrote:

> The air is melodious with the song of birds, a gentle breeze gives motion to the foliage and a full suggestion of *Life*. The faint hum of insects is soft as aeolian music, and the sound of the waters of a beck rushing down to the lake some little distance off seem to fill a sustaining tone in the symphony of *Nature*. The note of the cuckoo sounds bell-like and clear, and a thrush is singing its song of *Love*. Above – the sun shines down from a sapphire sky, while masses of pure white cloud hang here and there in forms of wondrous grace and *Beauty*. Below – slopes the garden, and beyond lies the calm and lovely *Lake* – the further shore of which is a perfect study of shades of green as the shadows of the clouds pass over the *Hills*. Away – towering up in the distance, is the purple summit of Coniston Old Man, with the broken outlines of Wether-Lamb, Crinkle Craggs, Bowfell and the Langdale Pikes silhouetted against the *Sky*. Truly a place in which to rest and be *thankful*.[44]

Simpson also brought his Kendal workers to Gill Head recording on September 1894;

> Our workshop party which circumstances have prevented us holding for two years took place today. A charabanc brought the party from Kendal to Gillhead [sic] after a row on the Lake, tea was partaken of indoors. The weather was all that could be desired. The evening, till dusk was spent on the Lake ... and the younger members of the party in bicycling, netting etc etc and after singing Auld Lang Syn a drive to Kendal by Windermere concluded a very pleasant afternoon.

The entry was signed by nine workers and three of their wives.[45]

One set of visitors, recorded two years later leave a more poignant reminder of times past. Through Jane Simpson's nursing connections and in particular her friendship with Honora Oddy, a District Nurse, Gill Head was host to a number of children from the Kendal

Workhouse. Simpson recorded the occasion in the Visitors' Book on 16 June, 1896.

> Through the kindness of Miss Oddy in collecting, and many friends in contributing money towards the drive, we were able to have the majority of the children from the Kendal workhouse at Gillhead [sic] for the day. They arrived about noon in a chara-banc with four horses and after lunch on the grass in the Orchard games were started and greatly enjoyed. A fire by the Lake to which all contributed fuel, gathered in the wood, boiled the kettle; and tea on the beach. A great quantity of weak tea and many buns were consumed and after a 'sweet scraffle' the drive to Kendal was resumed at 7.30 amidst much cheering from the children.

On a page, much inkier than the rest of the entries, twenty six names were recorded; four of them simply by leaving their thumb prints.[46]

It was, however, in response to his own growing children's educational needs that the School at Gill Head finally closed in 1900. Still mindful of the potential custom to be made from visitors and discerning tourists Simpson acquired premises in nearby burgeoning Windermere.

'The Handicrafts', the shop in Windermere

At Whitsuntide in 1901, 'The Handicrafts' shop in Church Street, near to the railway station, opened for business and for a while the family lived in the rooms above. The showroom here was used to

Arthur Simpson drawing in his workshop.

display items of woodwork alongside other sympathetic products made by local craft workers including metalwork, pottery, needlework and textiles; some, it seems likely, were from the Carlisle firm of Alexander Morton & Co. When James and Beatrice Morton had married, their son recalled; 'The bulk of the furniture for their first house dining-room, living-room and bedroom pieces, bought early in 1901 – was designed and made in solid oak by the crafts-man cabinet-maker, Arthur Simpson of Kendal'. Jocelyn Morton perceived the influence of Voysey in Simpson's work, with 'the characteristic dull beaten-copper handles, hinges and other fittings ... manufactured by Richard Rathbone of Liverpool'. It was, however, while Beatrice Morton (née Fagan) was a student at the Charlotte Mason College, one of Simpson's many teaching venues, that she, herself, had been taught the art of woodcarving by the visiting 'Professor'. Her skills had, in turn, enabled her to run her own classes 'from models by A. W. Simpson ...' which had clearly impressed one of her pupils, James Morton.[47]

There is, however, very little documentation concerning this five-year retail venture in Windermere when the main business of carving and furniture-making had continued to thrive in Kendal. In 1896 the Simpson firm left Berry's Yard and moved to the Queen Katherine Buildings where they were to stay for the next twenty-five years.

Queen Katherine Buildings

Situated just off Stramongate in Kendal, between New Road and the river, this was a large rambling building, which also housed three other businesses. Here the Simpson firm occupied the first and second floors until they were also able to rent the ground floor in 1919. The showroom was above the entrance in a room with a large bay window with the timber store, the polishing room and the fuming cupboard also on this floor. The workshops and offices were on the second floor, with the carvers taking advantage of the light provided by the three windows. Next to the cabinet maker's shop was the stoving cupboard, the warmest area of all where the timber was kept for at least a week before it was worked. Wood had generally been seasoned by being left for five years once cut, and then for seven years as planks, before it was used. A junior apprentice had the responsibility of stirring the sizzling glue-pot.

With no precise record books it seems, from contemporary photographs, that around a dozen men and one female clerk worked here in the early days. The hub of activity, as remembered by a 1921 apprentice, was clearly centred on the cabinet workshop:

A row of benches stood, one behind the other, in the traditional manner, with the men and the boys having the light from their left. Each hand had his own tools in his box under a window. Space was available to the right to allow for assembly of furniture. Under a window on the opposite wall, overlooking the yard, stood Tom Dixon's lathe and the bicycle fret-saw. There was no powered machinery at all until after the 1914 1918 war; many an apprentice went home with aching legs from pedalling the lathe for Tom. An extension from the roof from this shop, into the yard, provided shelter and the necessary gantry for lowering goods onto a wagon below.[48]

The Simpson Shop Drive to Longsleddale in 1908. Ronald, in the doorway, stands behind his mother Jane, with Thomas Dixon next to her. Hubert kneels second from the left with A. W. Simpson standing behind him. Top right is Arthur Dixon and to his left the 'tyrannical Bill Philipson'. Hilda is to their right, complete with pigtails.

Besides the shop in Windermere, it appears that in 1899 the family still had a home base in Kendal, at 7 Greenside. This was also the year that the ten year old Hubert Simpson began to keep a diary in which he recorded his first visit to the Art School and that Mr Voysey came to tea. His references to the workshop also imply that this was the year that the fourteen-year-old son of Tom Dixon, also named Arthur, began his apprenticeship with the firm. Five years later Hubert was to join him at the bench, after attending the Friends' boarding school at Ackworth in Yorkshire. No exceptions were to be made, however, for the boss' son by the 'tyrannical Bill Philipson'.[49] Hubert, like his father, was to spend time working and gaining experience in other workshops around the country before he returned to Kendal in 1908. In 1909 his diary records the many

events relating to his own developing role within the firm as well as his public commitments associated with the Friends. In 1910 he reached his twenty first birthday and officially completed his apprenticeship. His diary entry recorded cautiously that the men had been on short time but that the work had picked up and included an 'Order for desks from Voysey'.[50]

Ronald, Simpson's second son, completed his education at Ackworth two years after Hubert. Having shown a clear ability in art and design, he was to follow a different path, and spent a year under the tutelage of Collingwood at University College, Reading. His tutor reported, 'I send your boy back with great regret. He is quite one of my best students'.[51] In Kendal, he spent a year working at his father's business, designing and sketching furniture as well as doing some carving. Ronald left to join the firm of Alexander Morton in Carlisle, originally for only a few months, but became the 'young designer [who] produced many original designs, mostly for the firm's early printed ranges, and other important decorative work for the firm, including the first advertisements for the new 'Sundour' fabrics'.[52] He was to stay with them for the rest of his working life. The connection between the two family businesses was thus cemented.

In 1905, the showroom at Windermere was closed, but the title of 'The Handicrafts' had become so synonymous with Simpson's business that the sign was added to the Queen Katherine Building and from then on formed an intrinsic part of their address. The products of other craft workers were again displayed alongside the domestic furniture and carvings in the Simpson showroom, complying with his earlier intentions regarding 'the entire fitting of houses in an Artistic and Economical manner'. In 1909, however, this took on a more personal significance with the building of his own new family home.

Littleholme

> It was a small, almost square house, with a steeply pitched roof and a central chimney so that it looked like a house in a child's drawing. It was designed and built of local stone, without a trace of white roughcast and Voysey sheltered the front door within a wide arched porch, which must surely have been influenced by Charles Harrison Townsend's arched entrances to the Bishopgate Institute (1892–4) and the Whitechapel Art Gallery (1899–1901) in London ...[53]

In deciding to build a new family home it was not surprising that, as a proponent and practitioner of the Arts and Crafts Movement,

Simpson should chose his personal friend, C. F. A. Voysey, who was one of the most significant architects and designers of the period. Their first meeting at the proposed site on Sedbergh Road, in Kendal, was held on 19 June 1909 and clashed with the annual shop party, which Simpson was regrettably forced to forego. In essence the house was designed and pegged out before Voysey left for London two days later. Kendal Corporation approved the formal plans on 14 September and the work was contracted to the local builder J. W. Howie, with the first sod being cut by the family a few days later. Voysey was to make many visits to the site and by February the central chimney flues were near completion and Mrs Simpson was supervising the planting of fruit trees. An ingle fireplace framed by large curved pieces of oak dominated the sitting room and was photographed for the family Christmas card in 1910. Within it Simpson had designed 'a drop-leaf desk fitted with stationery compartments and drawers to the left of the fireplace for himself and a cupboard for Jane's sewing on the right hand side'.[54] This work was undertaken by Hubert Simpson.

When the family moved in on 16 June 1910, however, the work was by no means complete;

> ... only three doors were hung by then, the front and back doors

Littleholme *c.* 1911, the Simpson's Kendal home designed by Voysey in 1909.

> and one for the lavatory. Hubert had returned to give a hand with the move, spent the best part of June 17 waxing the beautiful oak sitting room floor. In the evening they were visited by several young friends who, with polishing cloths tied round their dancing pumps, helped to finish the job.[55]

The floor, oak fittings, and in-built cupboards were supplied by another Kendal firm, Hayes and Parkinson, although much of the work, including of course the furniture, was Simpson. This included a refectory table made by Wilfred Smith in 1908, a new writing desk and some items designed especially for daughter Hilda's small bedroom.[56] With the exception of the sitting room, the ground floor was covered with Staffordshire Stable tiles, with narrow rectangular green tiles used for the skirting. These co-ordinated with the tiles on the windowsills. The metal work, including the door hinges and the fenders around the fireplace, was made by the local blacksmith, Mr Winder. The house was lit by gas and Hubert, not Voysey, designed the carved escutcheons of the light switches. Not everything that Voysey had designed was to Mrs Simpson's liking, for despite his reputation for detail it was deemed that: 'The sink in the kitchen at "Littleholme" was so low that no-one but a midget could use it in comfort; there was no toe space below either'.[57] In 1911, when the architect visited the house, he found Mrs Simpson had deviated from his original specification and instead of red curtains she had chosen a 'Sundour' fabric, also adding some rugs from the Morton collection to add warmth to the floors. Despite these subtle criticisms he remained staunch in his beliefs, as conveyed in a letter to Simpson in 1918 that; 'No doubt the women can be very useful in suggesting many details. But their sense of proportion is generally wrong – they attach undue importance to trifles and forget the bigger things'.[58]

Many years later when discussions about extending Littleholme were held with the architect, Voysey expressed misgivings about the effect this would have on the original building. For whatever reason the changes were not implemented. A later letter, dated 2 March 1923, relating to such matters reflected the non-commercial nature of this particular commission and Voysey's on-going regard for the Simpson family, after his friend's death. He wrote

> There is nothing for you to pay me of course. I am pleased to help you if I can and would give you a detail drawing for the panelling or other partic[ular]s of which you have not already got the drawings.
>
> Yours sincerely,
> C. F. A. Voysey[59]

There seems little doubt of the close bond between the two men and whereas Voysey's character was most commonly portrayed in contemporary accounts as somewhat aloof, he was a generous host to his friend from Kendal. The two men often dined together when Simpson was in London for exhibitions or to buy timber. Their friendship and working relationship seems strangely to be reflected in the house they were to create in Littleholme. 'Although the house was designed as a simple artisan's cottage ... Voysey sheltered the front porch within a massive stone arch, which was surely inspired more by American architecture than by vernacular tradition'.[60] The porch, which was 'almost a quarter of an otherwise simple flat elevation was more pronounced and Voysey framed the opening with a heavy oak canopy'.[61] It reflected the simplicity and strength both men sought to encapsulate in their own designs and despite its modest brief it was reviewed in such prestigious trade press as *The British Architect*, *Architectural Review*, *The Craftsman* and in Germany, in *Moderne Bauformen*.[62]

In contrast to the somewhat sophisticated and austere picture created of Voysey, remembered superficially for his dapper way of dressing with the ubiquitous Liberty cravat, a distinction shared by his northern friend, it is easy to perceive Simpson as the more gregarious and outgoing of the two. Simpson, in his friendships with other contemporary Arts and Crafts Movement figures like Collingwood, seemed to enjoy nothing more than simple outdoor pursuits and family life. The presence of a letter from Voysey, however, discloses something more of the affinity that these two seemingly different men were able to share. Unfortunately, in what must have been an intimate sharing of feelings, only Voysey's side of the correspondence remains. Here he revealed:

> I often feel the loneliness you describe, especially do I feel that want of a sympathetic enjoyment of the beautiful. Though a member of the top Arts Club in the top Metropolis of the world, yet I am alone without one soul in whom to confide and with whom to enjoy truly the beauty of man made things. [63]

Both men would be tested further, personally and economically, in the changing world of the early twentieth century. For Simpson, came the challenge of a prolific workload, which like William Morris seemed to hasten his demise, as he dealt with the consequences of the outbreak of World War One.

The War Years of 1914–18 and their legacy

Like his father before him, on completion of his apprenticeship, Hubert Simpson began working as a journeyman in other parts of the country. By 1911, however, he had returned to Kendal to take up a more active role within the family firm. At this time 'The Handicrafts', as it was more generally known, was also selling the textiles and carpets produced by Ronald's employers, the Morton Co. As a result of this broadening remit, the Simpson firm was chosen as one of only fifteen designers and furniture makers to be awarded a stand at the third Ideal Home Exhibition. Hubert was given the responsibility for the exhibit, which was 'designed for an Evening room for work, reading and the evening meal'. As an endorsement of the quality and success of the project, the whole exhibit with some small exceptions was sold to one customer. Further evidence of an adjustment to the new age was the installation of the telephone at the Queen Katherine Building in 1912. In the same year a work cabinet made by Arthur Dixon and carved by apprentice Ernest Oldcorn was accepted by the Arts and Crafts Exhibition Society. Honours continued in the shape of Simpson's election to the Art Workers' Guild in 1913 and then later his award of a gold medal for a carved panel of an iris at a Paris exhibition.[64] This was one firm seemingly bridging the gap between the quality of individualism exalted by the Arts and Crafts Movement and the changing realities needed for commercial success.

St Margaret's Church in Prestwich, near Manchester contains a wealth of commissions undertaken by Simpson's firm including the Altar and Reredos, designed by Dan Gibson, which extended the length of the East wall. The illustration shows a part of this, which also included a delicately carved crown of thorns suspended from a wooden nail.

However, the outbreak of war disrupted production at Simpson's firm in Kendal, as it did with so many businesses. Both of Simpson's sons, like all eligible members of his work force, enlisted. Simpson himself was to serve as Secretary to the Kendal Committee for Belgian refugees, some of whom were given a room at the firm and with the wood provided were able to make and then sell clogs, amongst other things, on Kendal market. Mrs Simpson and Hilda worked with the female refugees in finding clothes, food and supporting them in other domestic duties as well as encouraging needlework skills. Simpson, perhaps not surprisingly, was also a member of the Tribunal set up to consider the question of individual military exemption on the basis of conscience. He was on Committees of the Society of Friends and continued with his work on the Council responsible for the somewhat turbulent Starnthwaite Home Colony, housed in and around the one time paper and bobbin mill near Crosthwaite, west of Kendal.

This colony, also known as 'The Westmorland Commune', was founded in 1892 by Herbert V. Mills. As a minister with the Unitarian Chapel in Kendal and author of *Poverty and the State* his hopes had been that 'the colony at Starnthwaite Mill will become a small Utopia of great beauty'. Such a project attracted Simpson's interest and it was also successful in bringing a number of people back to the land, including some 'unemployed socialists from Kentish Town'. Their ideas of democratic community living, however, conflicted with the somewhat autocratic style of Herbert Mills. The subsequent eviction of three of the colonists from the Community farm heralded Mills' own departure in 1901 when the estate, by then more renowned for 'its fruit than for its socialism', evolved into a reform institution. The administration for the colony had been placed under the Christian Union for Social Service, with a council which included both Arthur W. Simpson and Hardwicke Rawnsley, aimed to provide training for men from the workhouses in the hope that they would gain self-respect and become self-supporting. This, as the local *Bulmer's Directory* described would be the result of

> ... the healthy influences of a simple country home with the varied and interesting labour on the land, combined with a pleasant social life and a wise and loving discipline.

The task was formidable and by 1903 the mill was used more specifically as home to a number of epileptic boys placed there from workhouses around the country. A Boy Scout Troop was started and Lord Baden Powell visited them in 1915.[65] Simpson's alliance with such an ideal is both admirable and understandable but such a commitment only heightened the demands already placed on his time.

Those still working at the firm in Kendal now only included the long-serving Tom Dixon, the formidable foreman Bill Philipson and the clerk Miss Tanner, as well as some young apprentices. The bulk of the responsibility for designing, costing and all the travelling rested with Simpson. He was also involved with the new Design and Industries Association and gave a lecture at their Manchester branch, which was published in *The Cabinet Maker and Complete House Furnisher.* [66] Work, as indicated earlier, was to increase with the new demand for the design and production of more and more memorials as the sad consequence of young men losing their lives in war. One of the first commissions had come from the Holt family when their eldest son, Captain Joseph Holt, died at Gallipoli in 1915. Besides a plaque in their local church of St Margaret's in Prestwich, they also commissioned a large carved wooden chancel screen as well as a figure of Joseph Holt which was carved by Aumonier's. This was to be part of the long programme of work carried out by the Simpson firm in this church over a thirty-year period.

The workload and subsequent cost to Simpson's health made it possible for Hubert to secure an early discharge at the beginning of 1919. It was agreed that he should take over the business side and as recorded in his diary; 'There was a tremendous back-log of work to do, not least the sorting and tidying of four years accumulation of "rubbish". Three hundredweights of waste paper were sold, for 24*s*.'.[67] Unfortunately, this included some of the original drawings that had been made for individual pieces.

The acquisition of the lease for the ground floor of the Queen Katherine Building in 1919 heralded a new home for the timber store together with the eventual installation of a circular saw. This was in response to the growing situation where 'work was pouring in for domestic furniture and church fittings, and an enormous number of war memorials ...'.[68] At least two of the cabinet makers and one of the carvers did not return to their benches after the war. Both Cookson and Oldcorn, however, were able to rejoin Parkin who, with the exception of Simpson himself, had been the only employed carver during the war. Nevertheless the strain on both father and son began to show and in October 1920 Simpson suffered from a stroke while drawing in his workshop. Although he made a partial recovery a subsequent stroke in 1922 precluded all but one visit to his firm's new premises.

With the expiry date for the lease on the Queen Katherine Building looming, Hubert Simpson took advantage of the low cost of two warehouses and a yard near the river which came up for sale at

The Tudor Café in Leamington Spa with furniture designed by A. W. Simpson *c.* 1911.

auction. These had previously been owned by Isaac Braithwaite, the Quaker and Kendal manufacturer, who had been one of the first customers to commission a number of pieces of furniture, from Simpson, for his new marital home. Plans were implemented to adapt the buildings to meet the needs of the Simpson firm and in May 1922 a canvas sign marked the new premises at The Waterside.

Arthur W. Simpson died on 8 November 1922. Early in the morning his son, Hubert, began constructing what is believed to be the only coffin ever made by the firm of Simpson's. 'Each man and boy had a hand in the making' the oak casket which was to take Simpson to his final resting place in the Friends' Burial Ground near Littleholme in Kendal.[69]

Conclusion

It is not accurate or fair to suggest that Simpson's death meant the end of the firm but it did mark the end of an era. The firm continued, as its ledger attests, with the support of senior staff like Philipson and Cookson and the good wishes of friends like Collingwood. He wrote to Hubert;

> I am glad you are keeping on the business ... don't doubt you will be able to carry on worthily of the name you inherit ... turning out

> fine work which has made 'The Handicrafts' so well known and respected.[70]

In many ways it was an awesome responsibility to take on, in a time when a changing economic climate was to mean less work, men had to be laid off and labour relations became difficult throughout the land. Working conditions for the Simpson apprentices, like other workers there, had meant no morning or afternoon tea break. During the 1920s they took part in a day release scheme when they attended the Technical School for four hours in an afternoon and still received full pay of around 2 shillings. Failure to achieve at least ninety percent in their attendance, for the five additional evenings at night school, resulted in the firm withdrawing its payment of fees. No such compulsion had been necessary when Simpson himself had served his time at Gillows and spent the evenings in drawing and designing at Lancaster Art School.

Although still sustained by some church commissions, the ledger for this time reveals not only the diminishing number of orders but also the increasingly disparate nature of the firm. Customers loyal to the concept of true craftsman, like Ann MacBeth, may have ordered a walnut door wedge and a workbox but in 1931 an entry also recorded her purchase of *Good Housekeeping*, some linen, antique tiles, tongs and some Wedgewood mugs.[71]

Hubert was to serve on a number of public committees in Kendal and both Hilda and he succeeded Arthur as members of the Starnthwaite council. Hubert became a member of the Red Rose Guild of Artworkers, which enabled him to exhibit work in Manchester, but there was no denying the effect of the slump in demand. In 1930 the death of Tom Dixon further reduced a sadly depleted workforce. The business struggled on for another decade, with Arthur Dixon as the main worker, but by 1941 the impact of World War Two led Hubert to record in his diary what was becoming increasingly inevitable. In November he wrote; 'Must close down, I fear and seek other work'.[72] The premises at The Waterside were used for storage and a small area maintained to allow Arthur Dixon to continue with his work while also teaching at the Grammar School and Allen Technical Institute. Hubert, who had been developing his flair as a photographer, found alternative work with the Westmorland War Agricultural Executive Committee during the war years.

In 1950 Simpson's widow Jane died, at the age of ninety, and Hubert had no choice but to sell Littleholme and dispense with the premises at The Waterside, together with the stock. The archive reveals that the sale of 'The Handicraft' equipment on 18 October 1952 released £363 1*s.* 6*d.*

The legacy, however, was to continue and furniture produced in the Simpson workshops now attracts attention from far afield when, on the few occasions, it comes up for auction. The prices may have horrified the man whose personal ideology extolled the virtues of simplicity and thrift but, as with other work associated with the Arts and Crafts Movement, the crafting of individual pieces remains and is still recognised and appreciated. As a newspaper article observed in 1929;

> Mr Arthur Simpson, of Kendal, does not make furniture he fashions it, slowly, tenderly, and with loving care. He spends days, weeks, sometimes months on a single bureau or chair, but, as Mr Simpson says, that chair *will* be here long after he is gone.[73]

Acknowledgements

In this work I am indebted and gratefully dedicate this chapter to the written and spoken words of Eleanor Davidson.

All photographs in this chapter are from the Simpson Family Archive and appear by kind permission of Eleanor Davidson.

Notes

1. H. Simpson, 'Woodmanship' *c.* 1912, Simpson Archive, Ref. WDX 515, Cumbria Record Office, Kendal
2. What remains of the archive is housed within the Cumbria Record Office or is kept as family records.
3. Eleanor Davidson, *The Simpsons of Kendal – Craftsmen in Wood 1885–1952* (University of Lancaster, 1978), p. 3.
4. Fiona MacCarthy, *The Simple Life, C. R. Ashbee in the Cotswolds* (Lund Humphries, 1988 edition), p. 12.
5. E. Davidson, *The Simpsons of Kendal*, p. 3.
6. These memories were recorded following a stroke in 1920 when Hubert encouraged his father to write down, as he himself did daily, incidents from his long career. I was extremely privileged to have these events read to me by one of Arthur Simpson's grand-daughters.
7. E. Davidson, *The Simpsons of Kendal*, p. 4.
8. Roger Bingham, *Kendal, A Social History* (Cicerone Press, Milnthorpe, 1995), p. 229.
9. E. Davidson, *The Simpsons of Kendal*, p. 5.
10. Ibid., p. 6.
11. Eleanor Davidson, 'A Century of Carving', *The Lady*, 16 November 1978), p. 777.
12. Cutting from Arthur W. Simpson' s scrapbook in the family archive.
13. E. Davidson, *The Simpsons of Kendal*, p. 7.
14. Ibid., p. 8.

15. Ibid., p. 9.
16. Ibid.
17. Ibid.
18. See Gillian Naylor, *The Arts and Crafts Movement* (Studio Vista, London, 1971), pp. 120–2 for further information on the relationship of these two organisations.
19. E. Davidson, *The Simpsons of Kendal*, p. 42.
20. *Kendal Mercury and Times*, 12 March, 1886.
21. E. Davidson, *The Simpsons of Kendal*, p. 43.
22. See especially Fiona MacCarthy's account of C. R. Ashbee in the Cotswolds in *The Simple Life*
23. Bingham, *Kendal, A Social History*, p. 230.
24. E. Davidson, *The Simpsons of Kendal*, p. 12.
25. Ibid., p. 32.
26. Ibid.
27. Ibid., p. 13.
28. Ibid., p. 33.
29. *The Westmorland Gazette*, 29 August, 1891, p. 2.
30. E. Davidson, *The Simpsons of Kendal*, p. 44.
31. *The Westmorland Gazette*, 12 May, 1888.
32. See chapter four 'The Keswick School of Industrial Arts', for more discussion on Harold Stabler.
33. E. Davidson, *The Simpsons of Kendal*, p. 33.
34. Ibid., p. 16.
35. Cf. F. MacCarthy, *The Simple Life*, p. 111.
36. H. D. Rawnsley, *The English Lakes* (James MacLehose & Sons, Glasgow, 1902), p. 146.
37. E. Davidson, *The Simpsons of Kendal*, p. 34.
38. The Gill Head Visitor's Book, held in the Simpson archive at Cumbria Record Office, Kendal.
39. Anthea Callen, *Angel in the Studio* (Astragal Books, 1979), pp. 166–170.
40. Record Book in the archive of the Keswick School of Industrial Arts held in the Carlisle Record Office.
41. Mrs Willingham Rawnsley, sister in law of Hardwicke, exhibited a chest made of acacia wood, decorated with brass-headed nails at the Home Arts and Industrial Exhibition in 1896. See A. Callen, *Angel in the Studio*, p. 169.
42. Simpson Ledger held at Cumbria Record Office, Kendal.
43. Wendy Hitchmough, *C. F. A. Voysey* (Phaidon Press Ltd, 1995), p. 98. 'The balusters were priced at 2*s.* 4*d.* each …', p. 227.
44. The Gill Head Visitors' Book, an entry dated 13 May 1894 under the title 'Whit-Sunday Morning – The Orchard – Gillhead'.
45. Ibid., 15 September, 1894.
46. See also Eleanor Davidson's account 'A Summer's Day Out from the Workhouse' in *Cumbria Lake District Life*, July 1978, pp. 207–208.
47. Jocelyn Morton, *Three Generations in a Family Textile Firm* (Routledge & Kegan Paul, 1971), pp. 173-176.

48. E. Davidson, *The Simpsons of Kendal*, p. 47.
49. Ibid., pp. 20–21.
50. Ibid., p. 22.
51. Ibid., p. 29.
52. J. Morton, *Three Generations in a Family Textile Firm*, p. 119.
53. W. Hitchmough, *C. F. A. Voysey*, p. 201.
54. E. Davidson, *The Simpsons of Kendal*, p. 40. and Fig. 110.
55. Ibid., p. 40.
56. Ibid., p. 41. Some items of furniture from Littleholme are now at Abbot Hall Museum in Kendal and displayed at Tullie House in Carlisle.
57. Ibid., p. 37.
58. Letter in the family records.
59. Letter in the Simpson archive in the Cumbria Record Office.
60. W. Hitchmough, *C. F. A. Voysey*, p. 213.
61. Ibid., p. 201.
62. Ibid., p. 203.
63. Letter in the Simpson archive in the Cumbria Record Office.
64. E. Davidson, *The Simpsons of Kendal*, p. 26.
65. Citations relating to Starnthwaite from Dennis Hardy, *Alternative Communities in Nineteenth Century England* (Longman, 1979), pp. 111–114. Further information about Starnthwaite appears in E. Davidson, *The Simpsons of Kendal*, p. 19. and was also kindly provided by a research paper (undated) by John Gavin.
66. E. Davidson, *The Simpsons of Kendal*, p. 27.
67. Ibid.
68. Ibid., p. 28. Citing Hubert's diary entry dated 27 November, 1919.
69. Ibid., pp. 18–19.
70. Ibid., p. 29.
71. Ledger kept in Simpson archive at Cumbria Record Office.
72. Cited in E. Davidson, *The Simpsons of Kendal*, p. 60.
73. Cutting from the *Leeds Mercury* 30/iv/29 in the Simpson archive in the Cumbria Record Office.

CHAPTER THREE

The Langdale Linen Industry

> ... I should not omit mention of the charming linen woven at Langdale. For some purposes it is very useful, as good linen for embroidering on is not easy to obtain ... The Langdale linen is, of course, hand-spun and handmade, and the flat silky thread gives a very pleasant surface; but owing to its price and fine texture, it is not always suitable for the purposes of large hangings.
>
> May Morris, 1893[1]

As the Langdale linen order book recorded Morris & Co. were amongst an esteemed list of customers which included Queen Alexandra, the Royal School of Needlework, the Scottish School, and Messrs Liberty, all of whom purchased linen from the small cottage in Elterwater which was the headquarters of the Langdale Linen Industry in the latter part of the nineteenth century. This chapter aims to retell what was essentially a revival of a regional tradition in keeping with Ruskin's teachings, which extolled the merits of rural crafts and vilified the outcomes of mass-production. In bringing back the domestic tradition of spinning and weaving to the Langdales, however, romantic ideals had to be married to organisation and the practical abilities of those involved. While its success, in terms of producing an elite product, can be measured by the above citation from May Morris, one of the most renowned designers and embroiderers of this period, personality differences existed and were to play their part in the development of this industry.

Before discussing the practical issue of how this industry came into being, I want to emphasis the special place hand-spinning and weaving held for some, in epitomising the contrast between past civilisations and the negative changes many associated with nineteenth century industrialisation and urbanisation. By returning to classical literature some, like Albert Fleming the instigator of this revived industry, found solace in a time when poets waxed lyrical about the skills of the individual spinner and weaver and artists paid tribute to them on the walls of Egyptian tombs. Such scenes were far removed from the grim realities of nineteenth century mills in Lancashire and Yorkshire where profit was all and conditions were poor. As Albert Fleming wrote, in somewhat allegorical mood:

> For 'the dragons with golden jaws, the virgin labor [sic] of her shuttle,'

> you shall have cheap Manchester goods; for the sweet singing of poets under blue skies you shall have the roar of ten thousand spindles under black ones; and for the wise women who spin and the men to whom was given wisdom to do the work of a weaver you shall have gangs of factory hands, their stagnant souls rotting in their pallid bodies, wan as ghosts beside Acheron, though you have a dozen acts of Parliament to prevent you over-driving them.[2]

In referring back to the poets Homer, Catullus and Ovid, Fleming observed that their words echoed a working knowledge of the craft and that frequently their footnotes proved more instructive than any of his contemporary handbooks. This observation serves as a reminder that spinning and weaving had been an intrinsic part of pre-industrial daily domestic life; essential and fundamental skills enabling individuals to clothe themselves and furnish their homes.[3]

This notion of self-sufficiency, which also included the bonus of selling surplus thread, was indeed a fundamental part of Lakeland domestic life up until the early part of the nineteenth century. In his comprehensive study, *Westmorland Agriculture 1800–1900*, Frank Garnett gave the example of a farm labourer who lived in the west part of the county at that time, where he worked for sixpence a day and some meat. To him spinning was not only a necessity but also provided an opportunity to supplement his wage. The labourer had stated;

> Till I was wedded I had wrought for my father, and had got clothes when I wanted them. We had always a few sheepskins for breeches and I used to spin during winter nights ... My wife spun flax and I carded and spun wool at nights after work, which she took occasionally to Hawkshead, which was then a noted yarn fair.[4]

Progress and fashion had popularised cheaper mass-produced fabrics and a preference for what Annie Garnett, founder of the linen industry in Bowness, described as '... novelty's sake, machine- made linens'. The old skill of 'home-spun' had consequently been rendered redundant, as had the custom of teaching young children how to spin in school.[5] The loss of this domestic industry around the Langdales had affected those least able to respond to the changing economic picture by moving to the towns to find work. These included younger women whose husbands worked in agriculture or local industries as well as the ageing indigenous population. Practical needs coupled with the ideological aims of the founder, Albert Fleming, combined in contributing to what became known as the Langdale Linen Industry.

Romantic myths and hard realities

Despite describing himself, in an American publication, as a spinner and weaver Fleming was a lawyer by training.[6] His disenchantment with the legal system and societal values, however, had been recorded as early as 1874 in a letter he wrote to John Ruskin. This letter, clearly part of an on-going correspondence between the two men, was later included in *Fors Clavigera* and commended to Ruskin's readers for 'most serious consideration'. Fleming's letter throws some light on his personality and concern for a society that was increasingly prioritising material wealth over individual life. Writing from an address in Broxbourne in Hertfordshire, Fleming questioned the merits of the latest Law Reform Bill and noted:

> From a careful survey of lately reported cases, I find I can run away with my neighbour's wife, seduce his daughter, half poison his household with adulterated food, and finally stab him with a pocket-knife, for rather less than £1000. Stabbing is so ridiculously cheap that I can indulge in it for a trifling penalty of £1. (See Southall's case) [a police court case of the time]. But woe be to me if I dare to encroach on my neighbour's land, prejudice his trade, or touch his pocket; then

A Scenic view across the Langdales with the slate quarry in the background.

> the law has remedies, vast and many, and I shall not only incur pecuniary penalties that are to all effects and purpose limitless, but I shall be made to suffer in person also.[7]

His concerns were also extended to the effects of the government's laissez-faire attitude to trade and the policy of non-intervention where market forces were all and conditions for workers were seen to be of scant importance. Fleming's views aligned him with such political commentators as J. S. Mill, Thomas Carlyle, William Morris and not least John Ruskin all of whom came to represent an increasing element of 'educated opinion'. Their concern centred on the cultural and moral consequences of capitalism for Britain as the economy shifted its dependence away from agriculture to one based on commerce and industry. Eventually they saw this trend leading to the depopulation of rural areas as people moved to largely new and hurriedly constructed urban housing; this was to become more of a reality following a period of agricultural depression in the 1880s. In order to counter this effect a number of associations were initiated, such as 'The Society for Promoting Industrial Villages', with the support of businessmen, social reformers as well as politicians from both major political parties. As the historian Martin Wiener has observed; 'In the world's first industrial nation, industrialism did not seem quite at home'.[8] Instead an allegiance to the myth of the 'rural idyll' persisted and found popularity in a large number of contemporary paintings and novels. The desire to return to something which was perceived as purer and simpler than urban living therefore ran concomitant, serving to undermine a strong sense of industrial progress. Consequently,

> The notion of revitalising the countryside carries a powerful humanitarian and patriotic appeal. For many people the consolidation of the rural economy was seen as the ideal vehicle by which urban squalor and rural depopulation might be controlled and national vigour maintained.[9]

Albert Fleming concurred with such beliefs and found inspiration in Ruskin's writings, particularly *Fors Clavigera.* Other literary associations also provided inspiration and it was not surprising that Wordsworth's poetic lament for the declining use of the spinning wheel in Westmorland should have a particular relevance when Fleming moved to the Lakeland hills, where he found many of his neighbours living in impoverished circumstances. Women, in particular, had suffered through the decline of craft industries and many had been left to the vagaries of seasonal agricultural work and Poor Relief. However, as Fleming was to observe;

> Your true North-country woman does not ask for alms; her back is too straight for that, and her breed too good. Give her honest work and she will do it. But what work? [10]

His family, Le Flemings, were well known in the area when Albert Fleming took up partial residence at 'Neaum Crag' in 1880. His home occupied a striking position 'on Little Loughrigg against the face of the rock, and commanded a magnificent view of Wetherlam, the old Man [of Coniston], Bowfell and the stately pikes ...'.[11] Inside the house he had found an old spinning wheel, described as broken, forgotten and useless but which, in occupying a corner in his dining room, drew much comment from passing guests, mostly in terms of its archaic quality in the now mechanised age of textile production. For many of his older neighbours, however, the spinning wheel had represented happy times and as one of them was to recall: 'In mother's day every woman spun, but when t'wheels died out the gude times went too; m'appen they'd come come back if t'wheels did'.[12] Another voice, that of Ruskin living within a six-mile walking distance at Brantwood, had for some time been 'eloquently beseeching English men and maidens once more to spin and weave'. [13] All these factors conspired to make Fleming resolve to do what he could to restore this lost craft.

In one account of events Fleming tells of an eighty-six year old woman, who lived nearby and having spun in her youth was able to teach him the craft on his own spinning wheel, once it was mended. It was, however, a slow process as he recalled;

> her old, rheumatic fingers made a beautiful thread, but my clumsy, modern ones produced a dreadful gouty string, all tangled lumps and knots ...[14]

After mastering the basic practicalities Fleming approached John Ruskin with his ideas for an industry which, not surprisingly, were greeted with approval. Others, however, were more sceptical and when questioned more closely by friends in terms of what exactly he intended to do, Fleming formulated his argument firstly in terms of philanthropy, namely 'to help my old women, otherwise helpless'. Secondly and more comprehensively, in aligning the industry with the creative element of the Arts and Crafts Movement, he wrote:

> to assert in a humble way the principles preached in a noble way by Mr Ruskin, that all lasting and honorable[sic] work is done by men's fingers and men's minds and not by steam power, and that hiring electricity to run your errands, or the sun to paint your portrait, or steam to weave your linen, will not give sense to your message, or soul to your face, or durability to your shirt ...

This in turn would lead to a better quality product whereby, as he stated, '... I want to have, and want others to have, an entirely honest linen that can be trusted, that I can hand down to my children after me'.[15]

To test local opinion Fleming then began a promotional tour around the Langdale area where he gained the support of 'some kind ladies [who] at once took up the cause with enthusiasm'.[16] However, before anyone else could begin work, the question of finding more wheels had to be addressed. Advertising and searches yielded only seven wheels, some from as far afield as Stornoway and the Isle of Man, all unfortunately in a somewhat dilapidated state. To repair and replace the broken pieces appeared to present too formidable a problem and so it was decided that the carpenter at Skelwith Bridge should be commissioned to make fifteen new wheels, replicating Fleming's original wheel, at a cost of fifty shillings each. Despite difficulties in reproducing the iron components of the mechanism the resourceful carpenter managed to complete the work in two months. Teaching could now begin but, as I have discussed elsewhere, the early years of the industry owed much to the input of another 'incomer'.[17] When Fleming had moved into Neaum Crag, as Hardwicke Rawnsley was to record;

> He invited Miss Twelves to come up from the south to help him to arrange his house and engage his servants, and act when his summer guests were with him as good genius of the household, and in his winter absence as neighbourly caretaker.[18]

She too was to be closely involved with the industry at Langdale, and in *her* account of events Twelves describes herself as self-taught and responsible for teaching the 'dales-folk' when the project began in 1883.[19] This then was the 'kind friend [who] undertook the pleasant but arduous labor [sic] of instruction', whom Fleming referred to, somewhat dismissively, in his American account published in 1889. Interestingly later accounts by Fleming completely omit any mention of her, either in terms of her contribution or by name. Five years after it had started Twelves was to leave the Langdale industry, as she wrote, 'in the hope of obtaining more independence and reliable support ...' and join the Rawnsleys to run a linen industry affiliated to the Keswick School of Industrial Arts.[20] Her role, however, as others were to attest, was to be crucial in establishing and managing the foundations of the Langdale Linen Industry.

The Early years of Practical Application

> If the renewed industry was fortunate in having as its originator a man who was an idealist and could by his facile pen make its prospects known to the public, it was fortunate in having a practical woman and a most self-sacrificing and indefatigable enthusiast for Ruskin's teaching at its head to carry out all the difficult detail of starting the workers and organising the industrial effort. No words of mine are needed to put on record what the Langdale Linen Industry owed in its first five years of uphill work to Miss Twelves.[21]

Both Fleming and Twelves were to describe their early frustrations in trying to master the basic principles of the ancient craft of spinning. It may have seemed simple to turn a lump of flax into a thread on a bobbin but co-ordinating the foot movement on the treadle while feeding out the flax with the hands or from a distaff involved maintaining a consistent tension to keep the wheel spinning. For Fleming, 'Everything went wrong: the wheel reversed, the thread broke, and the flax twisted itself up into inconceivable bewilderments ... [but] I persevered for three days till I could and did do it'.[22] Twelves, while recording that she mastered the technique herself without instruction, told a similar tale of wheels turning the wrong way and the yarn twisting itself into innumerable kinks and knots. Undeterred the classes began, with both Fleming and Twelves describing their involvement as teachers. Whether these occasions followed the example Fleming described from an ancient print, where the spinning mistress gathered the pupils around her in a circle, so that she could admonish them with a long stick if necessary, was not recalled.

The decision to work with flax and not wool was taken, as Barbara Russell was to record, 'after careful consideration' as it 'presented less difficulties [sic] both to the spinner and weaver'.[23] This decision was clearly influenced by the impossibility of complying with what in the past had been a three year apprenticeship when so many of the pupils here were already advanced in years. At Langdale they decided that as soon as a spinster seemed able, which was usually after about three weeks' instruction, she would be allowed to take home a wheel to begin her own domestic production.

Originally Fleming had hoped to carry out the whole process of growing the flax locally, harvesting, breaking, scutching, hackling, spinning, weaving and bleaching, as he wrote 'from the flax in the field to the sheet on the bed'; but this was not to be.[24] Instead he settled for the more pragmatic solution of importing ready-baled flax from Ireland which was easily transported from Whitehaven via Cockermouth. It was then distributed to the spinners who were paid 2*s.* 6*d.* for each pound of thread spun, making it possible for them to earn, on average, around 5*s.* a week. What level of quality control was invoked was not recorded although clearly not all the thread produced in the beginning was suitable for weaving. As one contemporary account observed:

> The first bobbins that reached the weaver were a marvel of variety. There were threads of such diverse qualities that they could by no means be used on the same piece of cloth, thread that was so unequal and rotten that by the time the weaver had examined, cut and joined and made it ready for use he had spent almost as much time on it as if he had spun it himself, thread bad beyond all possibility of utilisation.[25]

The same author also mentioned the evening visits that had to be made to outlying cottages as pupils struggled to produce a reasonable thread. Despite recording that two of the best spinners could spin a pound of flax a day, it would seem that initially the level of wastage was quite high.

Although much of the work could be carried out by out-workers in their own homes, space had to be found to house the loom, teach the spinners and provide a central place for managing the industry. Again Fleming had referred back to a classical text and recorded the Greek poet Horace's instruction that; 'Near the house let there be a spring of running water and a little wood close by' and in a nearby village he found such a place.

> It stands in Elterwater, close under the shadow of Langdale Pikes. On its front is blazoned the date 1692. It fulfilled all my wants. There rising at the back was the Horatian wood, all bright, when I first saw it, with daffodils and the earliest primroses. Elterwater Tarn lies in front, shining low in the sweet morning light, and there too was 'the spring of running water' dancing and foaming under Elterwater bridge.[26]

The cottage was secured with the help of a £200 donation to the venture. It seems likely that Ruskin was again investing money, as he did with the mill at Laxey in the Isle of Man, in schemes he wished to encourage. The cottage was renamed St Martin's, 'after the soldier saint whose aim in life was to clothe the naked and give warmth to the suffering' [27] in keeping with Fleming's desire to find a saint 'as opposite as possible to the apostles of modern progress ... that Manchester and Bradford honor [sic] with statues'.[28]

The next stage of the process, having produced the thread, was to find a loom for the weaving. During their searches Fleming was

Elterwater with St Martin's Cottage, the headquarters for the Langdale Linen Industry, on the left.

introduced to a firm in Kendal that had once relied on hand-looms before progressing to steam power. In their cellar the remnants of a loom were recovered, and although riddled with rust and worm all the components were carried to St Martin's for the job of restoration. The following morning 'a solemn council was held over it' which, in Fleming's absence in London, was led by Marion Twelves and included both the local vicar and carpenter. The task of putting together the various components seemed insurmountable until as Fleming recalled;

> ... the ingenious lady bethought herself of a certain photograph of Giotto's 'Weaving', from Campanile. This was brought; and so, guided by this precious example, much light was thrown on its proper adjustment, and it was at last duly erected.[29]

In the pre-industrial textile industry, weaving was mainly carried out by men while women combined their general domestic and childcare duties with the more flexible skill of spinning. Both Marion Twelves and her successor Elizabeth Pepper, however, were to become proficient weavers; but initially the weaving at Elterwater was undertaken by a retired weaver from Kendal. John Thursby, who had once woven linen for a living, 'was persuaded to live and work at St Martin's for the princely sum of 16/- [80p] per week'.[30] A warping mill and winder together with a number of tools and appliances were gradually acquired and the art of weaving with its own language of heddles, reeds, picks, beaming and warping became a familiar part of everyday conversation.

On Easter Monday, in 1884, the first yards of linen were produced and disappointingly it resembled uneven sacking in appearance. As Fleming recalled; '... the scoffers rejoiced greatly. I own it seemed terrible stuff, frightful in colour, and of dreadful roughness, with huge lumps and knots meandering up and down its surface'.[31] Despite this, once the coarse material with the horrible smell had been washed in soap and water, put through a mangle and bleached in the sun it was transformed into a soft, light and fragrant fabric. Fleming had resolved not to use any methods that would cause injury to his workers and so in order to bleach the material he adopted Homer's principle whereby, 'Sun, air and dew were our only chemicals: potent magicians they, changing by their sweet alchemy our coarse brown stuff into soft white linen'.[32]

The original plan had been to produce bleached linen for long-lasting sheeting, with Fleming recording his own involvement in having taken 'thirteen yards of this harsh stuff, made into sheets, boiled, mangled, and bleached it on the grass'. However, another remunerative market was quickly identified by one of their first customers. A woman involved in art needlework saw the potential of using the subtle tones of brown, grey and yellow as an ideal material background to brightly coloured embroidery threads. As Fleming recalled 'I placed on my drab-colored[sic] linen a gorgeous crimson tulip, and it glowed into still brighter flame of color [sic] ...'. Consequently, this lady was not only the first customer to buy twelve yards of linen at the cost of four shillings a yard but also the originator of another aspect of the industry. The fashion for producing decorated household linen, such items as portieres, chair-backs, antimacassars and teacloths alerted Fleming to what he called 'the laudable mystery of embroidery'. Not wishing to miss a market opportunity he 'enrolled a staff of about forty poor ladies' to produce finished work for 'ready sale'.[33]

Although Fleming's early account implies an active participation in this work, his partial residence made him a somewhat elusive figure. There is evidence that in 1884 he, like Rawnsley, joined the membership list of the Guild of St George. He was also involved, alongside Rawnsley, in other local preservation projects but remained one of the shadowy figures of the Lake District Defence Society in his role as one of the first joint secretaries. He was, however, as Michael Dowthwaite has observed 'less prominent than the others, only living in the Lake District for part of the year, but as a lawyer was a great help to the society'.[34] His role in the Langdale industry was predominantly that of originator and the one who conveyed its message to the public. His job was made easier by the boom in soft furnishings which in turn generated a substantial clientele which enabled him to record in 1889; 'I find people do want the Langdale linen, for without advertising or publicity I have orders from all parts of England for many hundreds of yards'.[35] A year later his report concluded by stating:

> We have two looms going, and about thirty women at work. The old weaver gets a fixed wage of 16*s.* a week and a good cottage rent free. The best of our spinners earn about 6*s.* a week. We make seventeen different kinds of linen, varying in price from 2*s.* 6*d.* a yard. The widest is 44 inches, and its price is 5*s.* 6*d.* a yard. Stout, durable sheeting (very white and soft) is our staple production, but we aspire to table cloths and body-linen by-and-by. All money produced by the sale of linen is paid into the bank, and the profits will be divided among the workers at the end of the year.[36]

This last sentence undermines the criticism that 'Langdale's skilled craftswomen were being paid over sixty percent less than their sisters elsewhere'.[37] In comparing the workers here with those in the London firm of Morris and Co., Anthea Callen overlooks the social and co-operative nature of this industry which went beyond payment by piecework. In the next section I want to look more closely at the women who participated in the industry when it was managed by the indomitable Marion Twelves.

Developing and Securing the Industry

> Not the least interesting part of the experiment was the social brightness brought into the lives of the villagers by the simple hospitalities of the Crag. Miss Twelves organised spinster teaparties, and the good old days of dale spinning-'does'[sic] once more returned.[38]

The first gathering of the newly taught spinners was held on Christmas Eve in 1883 and annual gatherings followed to review business and discuss problems. Besides these formal occasions the women who lived on the fells around Little and Great Langdale were to benefit in other ways. In her article on 'The Langdale Linen Industry', published in the *Art Journal* of 1897, Barbara Russell described an area where some seven hundred people lived on the fells and in the villages of Elterwater and Chapel Stile, which had developed around the slate quarries. Despite improved roads many of those living out in the isolated farmsteads, where their husbands worked as shepherds or quarrymen, had to endure long and lonely winter months. During her visit Russell had been impressed by the level of hospitality offered to her by the occupants of cottages where 'the woman's arm and woman's skill can contrive to produce the most exquisite cleanliness'. She had noted that while the furniture shone and that 'on the flagged slate floors the most fastidious could find no stain' there had been an absence of comfort and warmth; 'hardly a rug, cushion or curtain!'. It was in such places that the return of the spinning wheel was to be greeted with enthusiasm.

The annual 'Spinners' Tea', however, may have been greeted with trepidation by some, as it involved an interview with Miss Twelves. She, while inquiring whether there were any complaints or wishes to retire from the scheme was also empowered to confiscate wheels from any unsatisfactory spinners. The response of one spinner to such a threat was recorded by Russell as 'T'day tha' cums t'door will be locked!' and that for some 'that they would sooner part with their lives than their wheels'.[39] The local paper report of 'A Spinsters' Tea' held at Neaum Crag in 1886, is, nevertheless, of one that passed without incident. In recording the presence of some thirty spinners and weavers it continued;

> The accounts for 1885 were passed and audited, and Mr Fleming and Miss Twelves gave a general review of the work done for the year. It seems that there is a real demand for genuine homespun goods, for £220 worth of Langdale linen has been sold during the last year. Constant work has been given to a large number of women, and whatever truth there may be as to the depression of trade in general, it has not affected this little industry, for not only has it proved to be self supporting, but after wages, rent, and all other outgoings had been paid, there remained a little profit in hand, which was divided amongst the workers.[40]

Having concluded with the business, tea was taken and then a number of young men joined the party for dancing old fashioned reels. This, as the article observed, was another aspect of the enterprise which would have pleased Mr Ruskin. The party finished at around eleven o'clock 'with three cheers for Mr Fleming and Miss Twelves'.

More frequent contact was made once a fortnight by those involved in the industry as they visited St Martin's to return their spun thread, receive payment and take home more flax for spinning. It would seem that real joy and pride was felt by those with a new sense of purpose in their lives. As Russell was to observe of one spinner, she 'watched her face glow with an artist's pride as she showed the bobbins full of fine silk or flaxen thread, and told of the struggles she had had to get it even and fine'. The tendency to patronise and moralise, however, was never far away. If single lonely women were deemed to have gained from 'the joy and interest it had put into lives so destitute of all that goes towards making life enjoyable' then those who had husbands were even more fortunate.

> The married women are equally enthusiastic; and, perhaps better proof still, the husbands are more so, for the wheel has brought increased comfort and orderliness into many a home whose mistress is now found busily engaged by her own fireside, instead of gossiping besides a neighbour's.[41]

Hardwicke Rawnsley had also been mindful of the risk of idle chatter. He recorded that 'tea-parties' were 'not allowed to degenerate into mere gossipings, for many a passage from the poets and from Ruskin were read aloud, and the aims of the Brantwood prophet and his good wishes of the adventure were spoken of'.[42]

Marion Twelves was herself strongly influenced by Ruskin's teachings but saw her work in the Langdales as only ' a mere foundation stone laid in position as it were' in terms of fulfilling his principles. She recorded meeting Ruskin two years after the industry had begun at the home of his friend, Susan Beever:

> He came into the room with bright, joyous haste, and both hands extended to give her greeting for the New Year. Then he took mine in his kindly grasp, gave me a seat at his side, and talked unreservedly of his own aims and efforts, and disappointments in the past, as if years of friendship has existed between us, and this little item of village work was merely an outcome of many such interviews ...[43]

In justifying her decision to leave the industry at Langdale, in 1889, she indicated that there were three areas of dissension. Writing in the American publication for their National League of Handicraft Societies in 1903, she cited Ruskin's mandate in *Fors Clavigera* to all companions of the Guild that 'you come forward to be givers, not receivers in this human world – that you are to *give* [her italics] your time, your thoughts, your labour ...'. In working with your hands it is the importance of '*individual* [her italics]effort – not work deputed to someone else, and then claimed as your own, but a steadfast consistent example'. Lastly she appeared to be suggesting, though not accusing anyone of, some financial misdemeanour. In referring to the conscientious and precise accounting Ruskin adhered to for the Guild's funds, she was clearly offended that this practice was not universally adopted. As she wrote:

> Every class seeking public patronage and support, should be required to produce a yearly authenticated report, or balance sheet, and be under observation in the working, on similar lines to your National League of Handicrafts.
> Every worker's name and address should be required with exhibits, and kept in a register by all societies or communities promoting the sales of village handicrafts so called: that the actual worker may be communicated with *direct*, should occasion arise when such a course may be expedient. It should be *absolutely impossible* for people of independent means to enter and sell their work at an exhibition of village industries, in contravention of the principles of honour, honesty, and justice.[44]

Her sense of anger is still clearly felt in recording these words five years after leaving Langdale when she had resolved to obtain 'more independence and reliable support in carrying out what I considered (and still consider) to be Mr Ruskin's economic principles …'. In the absence of any precise records it is not possible to present the other side of this disagreement or indeed to be privy to any Minuted Committee meetings. Both the St Martin's order book and account book, which I shall refer to later are not precise documents. There is also no way to identify the exhibitor at the village industry who caused such offence; one wonders if it could have been Annie Garnett, whom she may have perceived to be a person of 'independent means'.[45] Perhaps most problematic for Twelves was the pressure to produce quantities of work, when for her the issue of quality and workmanship had been the priority. In moving to Keswick she hoped, as she wrote;

> … not to make a larger industry with an unmanageable number of workers under my control, but to more firmly establish in the scope within my power of concentration and distribution an example of what may be accomplished by individual effort, *not* how many yards of linen may be made and sold, but how what *is* done may influence and help the doers within these limits, and be the means of inspiring others to similar effort beyond them.[46]

This suggestion of outside pressure, to increase the quantity of goods for sale, might explain a reason for the later accusation, in the 1920s, that factory-made goods were being passed off as hand-made in the Langdales.[47] However, during her five year period as manager, there seems little doubt that Marion Twelves imposed a strong influence on the industry, demanding an exacting standard while also subscribing to Ruskin's theories on the individual nature and satisfaction each worker should gain from her work.

Both co-founders of this industry had been 'incomers' to the Lake District emphasising the notion that a somewhat philanthropic agenda was being imposed on their indigenous work-force. Fleming's and Twelves' work in the Langdales connected them to other associations involved in farming communities, which sometimes set out to move people from urban workhouses to the countryside but were in the main concerned to provide an economic alternative to Poor Relief. In 1889 the publication of a collection of traditional spinning songs entitled *Songs of the Spindle and Legends of the Loom*, with a foreword by Albert Fleming, had been dedicated to the Rev. S. A. Barnett and his wife 'who had done so much for the workers in East London' in finding them work on the land. Henrietta Barnett, the vicar's wife, was also a founder of Hampstead Garden Suburb, 'where so many back-to-the-land ideas flourished'.[48] This small and somewhat sycophantic volume, which was produced to promote and embellish the ethos of the movement, was the handiwork of Langdale inhabitants. As the prefatory note self-consciously declared:

> This little book is the product of *hand-work alone,* [sic] and we have chosen to produce it in this way because we wish to preserve in each copy, as much of that individuality and human interest, as the price at which it is offered will permit.[49]

In the light of Marion Twelves' concern regarding individual recognition it seems ironic that in this same year particular mention should be made of personal attribution in the production of this book.

> Further, as it is our conviction that a workman will not be so likely to put heart and soul into his labour, if the result of it is never to be known to the world as his, and as it is only right that honour should be given to whom honour is due, we have, as far as *possible given the names of all craftsmen and workers* [sic] concerned in producing this volume, and we hope and believe that the purchasers of it will feel a kindly interest in knowing the names of those whose united handiwork they possess. For this idea we freely acknowledge we are in great measure indebted to 'The Arts and Crafts Society'.[50]

Illustrations were drawn by Edith Capper, who was also responsible for those which accompanied the article in *The Girls Own Paper* as well as Fleming's discussion on the industry included in *Ruskin's*

Collected Works. The cover of the book, not surprisingly, was covered in linen; the weaver was named as John Thursby and amongst the spinners was Eleanor Hesket, mother of the subsequent manager Elizabeth Pepper. Mother and daughter were not only excellent spinners but proved worthy in taking up the mantle of management which allowed the industry to continue into the early 1920s.

Claiming the industry back

The 1891 census enumerator's books showed Elizabeth Pepper to be twenty-eight years old and the mother of five children ranging in age from seven years to five months. Her husband was a slater in the Elterwater quarry and her occupation was shown as housewife, not spinner, nor weaver, not even manager. This in itself illustrates the difficulty in identifying the women involved in the industry when for all sorts of economic and social reasons they prioritised their domestic duties, in line with the prevailing view, when describing their role. In her 1897 article, however, Barbara Russell confirmed that; 'The management of the spinning and weaving is in the hands of Mrs Pepper ... herself one of the first pupils, and now the best spinner and weaver in the whole district'. She also mentioned Pepper's mother, Eleanor Hesket, who was 'one of those, to whom the industry has been a real blessing, enabling her to keep her tiny home together without becoming a burden on any one' and therefore spared the stigma of seeking Poor Relief.[51]

The family home was a working farm at Holme Ground in

Elizabeth Pepper and her mother spinning outside St Martin's Cottage.

Tilberthwaite and from here mother and daughter made the three mile journey in pony and trap to Elterwater. At St Martin's cottage they attended to the everyday business of giving spinning and embroidery lessons, issuing and paying for the spun flax, sorting the bobbins, weaving, bleaching as well as dealing with the correspondence and the sale of small items of linen and embroidery, made for ready sale. St Martin's was well placed on the road between Coniston and Ambleside to attract passing trade from those walking in the Langdale Fells or staying at the recently extended village inn, aptly named Tourist's Rest. Some entries in the order book simply indicate sales to a 'visitor', as in the case of a spinning wheel sold in 1889 for £2 5*s*. More frequently, however, such sales related to pillow lace, pincushions and handkerchiefs.

Although Marion Twelves had laid the ground work it seems that Elizabeth Pepper's undeniable talent and skill expanded the range of goods produced in the Langdales. When John Thursby retired from St Martin's the thread used for making the basic sheeting and canvas was sent to an un-named Scottish weaver, while other linen thread went to John Bell in Ambleside. One entry in the account book, at the beginning of the 1890s, recorded a payment of £1 4*s*. for his week's wages. He, like Elizabeth Pepper also wove in a combination of linen and silk to produce a material, which was 'very beautiful in texture, not too costly, and delightful to wear'.[52] The same combination was produced at Bowness where Annie Garnett called it 'throwan'. Pepper also wove a fabric in pure silk, which was used traditionally as a contrasting background to show off the fine Greek and Ruskin lace. Although both red and blue were used, Pepper was known to favour a deep royal blue. It seems an attempt was made to make this a truly local product as Russell noted that silkworms were reared locally at Grasmere and that silk produced from them had been woven and sold in London. Verification of this may be difficult to establish, or perhaps believe, but Abigail Reed referred to one example of her grand-mother's work as 'backed with silk from silkworms'.[53] Annie Garnett also made reference to her attempts to grow mulberry bushes and rear her own silkworms in Bowness. The spinning of silk in the Langdales became an important element of the industry with as many as a quarter of the work force engaged in this activity. Much of this must have been used for the silk thread in the other increasingly successful side of the industry; the production of embroideries. Pepper's work and skill in this field was judged that 'for beauty of design and finished workmanship, [it] ranks with the finest needlework of any nation'.[54]

Besides using her own designs, the work of other designers were transferred on to the linen and despatched to local out-workers. In this way as Russell recorded;

> Quilts, cushions, cloths, and – exceeding them all, perhaps in beauty and usefulness – wall hangings, wrought simply or elaborately, but always with most finished art, are to be found in the Elterwater showroom, and at times at the various Art Exhibitions throughout the kingdom, where they gain prize after prize whenever entered for competition.[55]

The Langdale Linen Industry was also present in a prestigious list of exhibitors in the 1893 Arts and Crafts Exhibition Society, which included the Leek Embroidery Society, Morris & Co. and the Royal School of Art Needlework. Four cushions, designed by Heywood Sumner, the renowned designer, archaeologist, painter and etcher, were embroidered by Mrs Ward of Langdale, who also exhibited another of his designs, 'The Woodside', in 1903.[56] Mrs Pepper regularly attended the Home Arts and Industries Association exhibitions around the country as well as those held in the north. In 1897 they won fourteen awards at the Lancaster Arts and Crafts exhibition.

Besides embroideries and linen, Elterwater also earned a reputation for its lace, so much so that Russell remarked, 'some of its workers excel all other English lace-makers in its production'.[57] This was indeed a compliment as the cottage industry of Victorian lace making was considered to centre on Devon and the Midland counties of Buckingham and Bedfordshire; some of these areas had developed a particular tradition for the craft through the influx of Protestant refugees fleeing the low-lying countries of northern Europe in the sixteenth century. The Victorian fashion for accessorizing clothes with lace, however, was largely served by the mass-producing machines in Nottingham. Few hand-workers could compete in terms of price or delicacy. Their only chance was to exploit the individual artistic merit of what they could produce.

Greek, or what became known locally as Ruskin lace, for which Langdale and Keswick gained fame, was not simply named after the movement's great benefactor. Anecdotally it was believed that Ruskin was personally responsible for suggesting that such work could be reproduced in the Lake District. The lace, unlike traditional bobbin lace, was worked with a single needle in either silk or linen producing a durable decoration for household and ecclesiastical linen. Cutwork and darned work on a netted background added to the industry's range of products.

The question of who exactly was buying the Langdale textiles cannot be comprehensively answered. The St Martin's order book which spans from 1884 –1925 contains some names and instructions (not always legible) which are listed vaguely under the year but with no precise dates. This would seem to suggest that organisation of these commissions was under the control of one person. A separate account book was started in 1889, which may have been enacted to placate the concerns Marion Twelves clearly had about issues of financial accountability. Unfortunately, like the order book, it is not arranged in any ordered fashion but simply makes note of payments and postage costs. It does however, record that the cream for the Spinning Tea cost 2*s.* in 1895. After 1898 there are very few entries and gradually it peters out and seems to relate more to domestic items and lists of food. The reasons for such incompleteness may have been compounded by the suggestion that Elizabeth Pepper worked mainly from her home after 1901.[58]

The first customer to be recorded in the order book for 1884 was 'Mr Rawnsley', who bought 14 yards of linen and a tablecloth. Lady Bective, who had helped in the search for wheels and was to be a well-known patron of the local enterprises in the Langdales and Bowness, bought 3 yards of linen. Other early aristocratic clients included Lady Leigh who bought 84 yards of linen, and Lady Brownlow whose husband was the President of the Home Arts and Industries Association. Some time before 1886, 'Messrs. Liberty' ordered 41½ yards of linen, placing a further order for 40 yards in 1886. As indicated at the top of this piece Morris & Co. were customers, placing their first order for ten yards of 'excelsior' on 4 September and then a further order for ten yards of linen, which cost £1 15*s.* on 13 September 1889. Both Annie Garnett and Mrs Brownson regularly placed orders on behalf of the Spinnery, with a particular order placed in March for '30 yards of 21 inch linen

Elizabeth Pepper weaving at home. This photograph was used as a postcard to publicise the industry.

white' described in the back of the book as 'on hand on 12 June 1890'. The Spinnery orders ceased to appear around 1896. A. W. Simpson ordered 21 inches of linen on 13 November 1890 and paid his 2*s.* seven days later.

Linen was also supplied to the Scottish School and the Royal School of Needlework as well as to Montague Fordham's Gallery in London. The actress Ellen Terry placed two orders in 1893, one for 13 yards of linen for sheets and a later order for 26 yards of linen which, together with postage, cost £7 5*s.* 3*d.* Royal patronage was secured in 1901 when Miss Wolfe ordered 28 yards of linen 'dyed special' on behalf of 'her Majesty Queen Alexandra', who paid £10 10*s.* 0*d.*

Elizabeth Pepper used and experimented with traditional vegetable dyes which had once been used in the dyeing of wool. In keeping with Fleming's standpoint lichens, grasses, heather and logwood were all used to create a subtler effect on the linen than the harsher new chemical dyes. She also experimented with weaving and advanced her skills to include herringbone patterns. Her skills as a communicator were to include portraying the industry in verse. It began;

> In a little village 'neath the pikes
> There's some industrious people
> Aye, some that live beneath the shade,
> Of Brig Hows old church steeple.
> In passing quietly through the vale,
> You hear them gaily singing,
> You step aside and see them spin
> Fine thread of Langdale Linen.[59]

Her ability to communicate also made her a successful teacher, as Annie Garnett acknowledged when she engaged her to teach in Bowness. Further afield her grand-daughter recalled Pepper spending a month teaching some girls in a class in Sandringham and even more prestigiously, one of her pupils was to be Queen Alexandra. In retelling memories that were part of the Pepper family history it seems fitting to dedicate this next section to the personal writings of Elizabeth Pepper and events revealed through recordings made with her grand-daughter, Abigail Reed.

Family Memories

Besides her grand-daughter's memory of her stay in Sandringham, Elizabeth Pepper left her own account, in a very small black address book, of two visits she made there, firstly in 1897 and then again in

Elizabeth Pepper, complete with sophisticated headwear, attending her stall at the Home & Arts Industries exhibition held in London in 1906. She stands poised to take another order surrounded by an assortment of the Industry's products, including embroidered cushions, examples of Ruskin Lace and one piece bearing the message 'Make new friends'

1901. On the first occasion she had travelled, seemingly with her mother, to King's Lynn to take part in the Commemoration Trades & Industrial Exhibition which was held at St James Hall on 10 to 18 February. Mrs Pepper had arrived on the 7th, allowing plenty of time to prepare the stand of exhibits before the then Princess of Wales opened proceedings on the 9th. During 'a long chat' with the Princess about the Langdale textiles she was invited to visit Sandringham at the end of the exhibition. Subsequently on 14 February Mrs Pepper recorded:

> 14th am to Sandringham went to church saw the Queen's oldest daughter Empress Frederick, Prince & Princess of Wales & Princess Victoria and then to dinner after.
> For a drive with mother to see the cows & sheep & lambs & bulls. Oh so grand & then to see the stud where the Grand Prize Winner called Persimmon, such a beauty. Went to York Cottage [the Wales's country home in the grounds of Sandringham] & to Princess' dairy & saw the butter made for the dinner table at night for the Hall.
> Princess of Wales was there & Empress Frederick & Princess Victoria & [they] have 100 servants at the Hall.
> Sir Dighton Probyn [A member of the Royal Household & Keeper of the Privy Purse] much interested & said I was a real Royal Guest. The Princess smiles & bowed in the church & seemed much pleased, it was a nice visit saw many treasures but it was all to short a time ... [60]

Both this and a subsequent record were signed as if to verify the occasion. The next visit was somehow even more surprising, coming as it did only six days after Queen Victoria' s funeral. Mrs Pepper revealed that on 3 February 1901 she 'went to London to go on to King's Lynn Exhibition. Had an invitation to go to Sandringham'. One is left wondering whether she was among the throng of mourners on the streets of Windsor the day before. She makes no mention of this or any reference to the Queen's death. Although her writing is difficult to decipher it seems she again went with the 'Princess of Wales to [the] dairy to see the cows', a pleasure more esteemed visitors, such as Lady Antrim, also had to endure,[61] and then;

> Went out in Queen Victoria's Pony Carriage with Princess & Nurse carried Prince Eddie round Deer Park & back to York Cottage. Duchess of York, Princess Mary was pleased.
>
> L. Pepper

When asked how she thought her grandmother had got on with the Queen, Mrs Reed replied; 'Alright ... it was all part of the thing in those days ... you didn't know anything else – just ordinary folk'.[62] The visit had, however, instigated the purchase of a new hat and cape each recorded as costing 21*s*. Mrs Pepper also noted other expenses which included two rooms at 13/- per week, the train fare to King's Lynn at 8/½ [sic] with excess baggage costing 3/-. The reason for this expense is made clear by a subsequent payment of 2/- to a man to open and pack the looms into cases, equipment which had clearly been brought along for demonstration purposes. It seems likely that such expenses were countered by commissions placed at the exhibition including the aforementioned order of linen 'specially dyed' for the new Queen in mourning. The Queen's gift to Mrs Pepper of a spinning wheel was much treasured amongst a collection of wheels, which accumulated at Holme Ground, to be used by her mother and sister Mary Fell, (married to quarryman Robert Fell) in what seemed to become an increasingly family based enterprise. Certainly, grand-children Abigail (Reed) and her brother Robin were involved in the bleaching of the linen when it was laid out in the little paddock attached to the house where they had to water it. Kept in position with two stones at each end and two in the middle this memory brings to life the picture drawn by Edith Capper in *The Girl's Own Paper* showing 'open-air bleaching' and the description:

> At any time of the day groups of people might be seen gazing in rapt admiration at what appeared to be a big piece of calico laid upon the ground ... Once too every available piece of it was carried to a specially picturesque, but in truth remarkable rocky field, that there,

> amongst the very choicest surroundings, in full view of the stretch of the Langdale Valley and the misty blue mass of its Pikes, the linen might be bleached by the sun, and the wind, and the purifying dew.[63]

When asked how long it was left there Mrs Reed replied, 'Oh quite a while until it got to the right colour'. And what if it rained? 'It didn't rain'. You don't remember it raining [incredulous]? 'No' she laughed.[64]

Other ways in which the grandchildren helped included the picking of mushrooms and flowers that could be used for embroidery designs. Mrs Reed remembered, 'If she [Nana] saw say a buttercup in a field, we would have to get this blooming thing and then she would put it into a jam jar or something and work it onto linen ...'. When asked if her grandmother had received any formal art training in this, the reply was negative.[65] Mrs Reed also remembered seeing her grandmother dyeing things and the lovely effect this had on the linen. Lichens were used and the children were instructed to collect them from particular places; 'She used to say, did my grandmother, go to such and such a place'. Then the children would scrape it off the stones with a knife. When asked whether it was just lichens that were used on the linen, Mrs Reed replied; 'Lichen and white moss were the two things we used to collect. And the white moss ... [was used] to go for healing the wounds in the First World War. They used to send it abroad'. She confirmed that this was sphagnum moss and that 'there was a place at Holme Ground in a little meadow which was quite near home, which had a swampy sort of bit where there was a lot'.[66]

Four generations of spinners involved with the Langdale Industry: Eleanor Hesket, her daughter Elizabeth Pepper, her daughter Abigail Nelson and her daughter Abigail Reed.

Mrs Reed had learnt how to spin when she was around six years old, at a time when her grandmother worked in the room over the top of the coach house; she remembered 'in there was a lovely big room and she had a loom set up there'. Here Mrs Pepper wove the flax that came from Harrison's in Cockermouth but her granddaughter was a reluctant pupil-weaver explaining 'you know how it is when you're a youngster you don't want to be doing things like they want you to do'.[67] The volume of work may have been seen as daunting as she also remembered her grandmother working until two or three o'clock in the morning to complete and send off orders. When asked if she recalled any contact with Albert Fleming, Mrs Reed replied:

> [he] was a very good friend of my grandma's. She used to go a lot to Neaum Crag. And I've been many times with her ... my grandmother used to take him eggs and butter and whatever from the farm, you know. Just whatever he wanted, but it was a nice little spot to go to. And Miss Fleming [his sister] was especially nice ... She was just a little lady but ... Albert Fleming was a very forthright sort of a man from what I can sort of remember of him. I used to keep hold of my grandma's skirt ... it was sort of a bigish house, and everything, but he was very good ... very good with her.[68]

Life at Neaum Crag was clearly very different to that at Holme Ground where as in many of the Langdale farming communities diversity of employment was a necessity. Like her grandfather, Mrs Reed's father not only farmed at Holme Ground, he also carted slate to Coniston each day, returning on the six horse wagon with a load of coal. In the summer months the family income was supplemented by letting the cottage in the yard to holidaymakers who 'used to come from Barrow or Liverpool'. It was they and other tourists who would buy the smaller items worked on during the winter months by the women of the family including Mrs Reed, her mother, aunt and cousins. Her aunt Mary Fell (neé Pepper) was particularly adept at bobbin or pillow lace but it was all made to Mrs Pepper's design and instruction; 'she knew what she wanted'. The picture Mrs Reed portrayed of her grandmother, I suggested, was of a very strong woman. Mrs Reed concurred; 'Ah she was, she was alright was Nana'.

Conclusion

The last date in the account book is 1925 but the records before this date are sporadic to say the least. The suggestion that 'the final blow' hinged on an accusation that factory-made products had been passed off as hand-made cannot be substantiated.

The farmhouse at Tilberthwaite displaying the sign for 'The Langdale Linen Industry'.

The survey of 'Decorative Crafts & Rural Potteries', by Fitzrandolf and Hay in the post First World War years, indicated that rivalry existed between the Lakeland textile industries. Strong personality differences may indeed have played a part in this and the situation was possibly exacerbated by the publicity photographs of workers like Mrs Pepper in 'quaint rustic dress'. The suggestion exists that this 'reinforced urban notions of the idyllic rural existence of peasant craftswoman' and was used to attract tourists. The accusation then follows that this enabled them to charge higher rates for their produce than elsewhere in the country.[69] There is no evidence of this within the account book and certainly when Mrs Pepper attended national exhibitions, commissions would have been given in competition with similar industries. There remains, however, the possibility that within the local tourist trade someone could have exploited the situation by misrepresenting the origin for their own financial gain. It seems very unlikely that this was anyone close to Mrs Pepper, certainly Mrs Reed had no knowledge of it. Her view was more pragmatic;

> ... the war came and ditched the lot ... well of course it had to because all the men went into the army ... don't forget there was the farming to still be going on ... and then there was the baking and all that and there was all of us to look after.[70]

The war, as observed with other arts and crafts industries, changed the nature of what was produced. In the Langdales they made a very coarse linen that was used in the making of rucksacks for the troops. The finer work still remained a family skill but other opportunities were to open up for subsequent generations of women. Mrs Pepper's daughter Abigail attended Charlotte Mason's College with the intention of becoming a teacher but this was interrupted by the war which made her presence necessary back at Holme Ground. Her daughter, Mrs Reed, however, was to leave the farm to find work in Kendal, firstly with the Clarke family and the workhouse and then for the local council. She, like other family members, continued to produce work for domestic use as well as ecclesiastical pieces for the churches at Allithwaite and Flookborough. The continuation of this craft endorses Barbara Russell's view that such work 'is no mere experiment, but has an intrinsic value of its own to all who can appreciate beauty of texture, colour and fine needlework'.

The Langdale Industry was indeed to prove particularly resilient and also become 'the parent of other similar industries, every one of which owed its original inspiration to the success of the experiment at St Martin's'.[71] In Gloucestershire and Wiltshire and closer to home in Keswick and Bowness its ethos had found endorsement. Much of that success, however, must be attributed to the individual work and contribution of the personalities involved. Both Marion Twelves and Annie Garnett, as shown in other chapters, were capable and effective managers. Mrs Pepper, in sustaining the linen industry firstly at St Martin's in Elterwater and then at Tilberthwaite, demonstrated equal ability and determination. Her skills as a craftswoman and communicator enabled her to broaden her rural horizons and made her 'very proud' to meet with those from the very highest echelons of society.

Albert Fleming, who with John Ruskin, had been the central male figure in initiating the industry, died in 1923. He had returned to make the Langdales his permanent home after his retirement from Gray's Inn. His obituary paid tribute to his artistic and literary merit and described the final service when his ashes were scattered.

> On Sunday morning a number of his personal friends and neighbours assembled on the rocks on Little Loughrigg – which are reached immediately from the grounds of Neaum Crag – for the purposes of carrying out his last wishes as to the disposal of his ashes, as these rocks had been chosen by him for the final obsequies. Here a small altar had been erected, and a special service, compiled by himself, was read.[72]

The singular nature of this service echoed the sentiments he and many others felt in aligning themselves with the Lake District landscape. His social conscience found practical application in helping the women of the Langdales. In his thinking and for his inspiration

Fleming, however, had no doubt to whom he was indebted. In acknowledging the importance of John Ruskin and his philosophy, he wrote: 'To him I owe the guidance of my life, – all its best impulses, all its worthiest efforts …'.[73]

Acknowledgement

All photographs in this chapter are from the Abigail Reed Archive and were kindly supplied by John Marsh.

Notes

1. May Morris, 'Of Materials' in *Arts and Crafts Essays by Members of the Arts and Crafts Exhibition Society* (Thoemmes Press, 1996 edition), p. 371.
2. Albert Fleming, 'Revival of Hand-Spinning and Weaving in Westmoreland [sic]' in *Century Magazine*, USA, February 1889, p. 522. I am grateful and indebted to Alan Sykes for a copy of this article.
3. B. Pidcock, 'Domestic Textile Production in the Sixteenth and Seventeenth Centuries' in M. Winstanley (ed.), *Rural Industries in the Lune Valley* (CNWRS, 2000), p. 23.
4. F. Garnett, *Westmorland Agriculture 1800–1900* (Titus Wilson, Kendal, 1912), p. 93.
5. Annie Garnett, *Notes on Hand-Spinning*, (Dulau & Co., 1896), p. 12. See also A. Garnett, *Windermere Industry at the Spinnery, Fairfield, Windermere*. More discussion on her business in Chapter Five.
6. A. Fleming, 'Revival of Hand-Spinning and Weaving in Westmoreland', p. 521.
7. Cook and Wedderburn (eds), *The Works of John Ruskin* (1907), 'Fors' vol. 28, p. 141.
8. Martin J. Wiener, *English Culture & The Decline of the Industrial Spirit 1850–1980* (Cambridge University Press, 1981), p. ix.
9. G. Spenceley, 'The Lace Associations' in *Victorian Studies* vol. 16 (1973), p. 434.
10. A. Fleming, 'Revival of Hand-Spinning and Weaving in Westmoreland', p. 522.
11. Description from the obituary of Mr A. Fleming which appeared in the *Westmorland Gazette* on 31 March, 1923. Again my thanks to Alan Sykes for a copy of this and Fleming's will.
12. Ibid.
13. A. Fleming, 'Industrial Experiments in Connexion with St George's Guild' in Cook and Wedderburn (eds), *The Works of John Ruskin*, vol. XXX (1907), p. 328.
14. A. Fleming, 'Revival of Hand-Spinning and Weaving in Westmoreland,' p. 522.
15. Ibid., p. 523.

16. Ibid., p. 524.
17. Jennie Brunton, 'The Late Nineteenth Century Revival of the Langdale Linen Industry' in E. Roberts (ed.), *The Linen Industry in the North West* (CNWRS, 1999), pp. 93–118.
18. H. D. Rawnsley, *Ruskin and The English Lakes* (James Maclehose & Sons, Glasgow, 1902), p. 137.
19. M. Twelves cited in F. A. Benjamin, *The Ruskin Linen Industry of Keswick* (Michael Moon, 1974), p. 27.
20. Ibid., p. 28. See Chapter 4 for more details on her career after she left the Langdales.
21. H. D. Rawnsley, *Ruskin and The English Lakes*, p. 137.
22. A. Fleming, 'Revival of Hand-Spinning and Weaving in Westmoreland', p. 523.
23. B. Russell, 'The Langdale Linen Industry', in *Art Journal* (1897), p. 330.
24. A. Fleming, 'Industrial Experiments in Connection with St George's Guild', p. 329.
25. Unattributed article, 'A Restored Industry', *Girl's Own Paper*, vol. XV, No. 762, 4 August, 1894, p. 691. My thanks to Meg and Martin Riley for this.
26. A. Fleming, 'Revival of Hand-Spinning and Weaving in Westmoreland', p. 525.
27. M. Blake, *Revival of Spinning and Weaving in Langdale*, Langdale Series, 1976, p. 6.
28. A. Fleming, 'Revival of Hand-Spinning and Weaving in Westmoreland', p. 525.
29. Ibid., p. 526.
30. E. Prickett, *Ruskin Lace and Linen Work* (Batsford Ltd, 1985), p. 10.
31. A. Fleming, 'Industrial Experiments in Connection with St George's Guild', p. 329.
32. Ibid., p. 330.
33. A. Fleming, 'Revival of Hand-Spinning and Weaving in Westmoreland', p. 527.
34. Michael Dowthwaite, 'Defenders of Lakeland: The Lake District Defence Society in the Late Nineteenth Century' in Oliver Westall (ed.), *Windermere in the Nineteenth Century* (CNWRS, revised edition 1991), p. 53.
35. Ibid.
36. A. Fleming, 'Industrial Experiments in Connection with St George's Guild', p. 330.
37. A. Callen, *The Angel in the Studio* (Astragal Books, 1979), p. 117.
38. H. D. Rawnsley, *Ruskin and The English Lakes*, p. 142.
39. B. Russell, 'The Langdale Linen Industry', pp. 330–1.
40. Cutting found in the K.S.I.A. archive, Carlisle Record Office, DB/111/93 inscribed 19 February 1886.
41. B. Russell, 'The Langdale Linen Industry', p. 331.
42. H. D. Rawnsley, *Ruskin and The English Lakes* , p. 142.

43. Cited in F. A. Benjamin, *The Ruskin Linen Industry of Keswick* (Michael Moon, 1974), p. 28.
44. Ibid.
45. See Chapter Five.
46. Cited in F. A. Benjamin, p. 28. See Chapter Four to follow the development of her work with the Keswick School of Industrial Arts.
47. H. Fitzrandolph and M. D. Hay, *The Rural Industries of England and Wales*, Part III, 'Decorative Crafts & Rural Potteries' (Clarendon Press, 1927), p. 90. where in their survey they suggest the collapse of the industry followed when one weaver was exposed for selling factory made goods.
48. Jan Marsh, *Back to the Land* (Quartet Books, 1982), p. 132.
49. H. H. Warner (selected and arranged), *Songs of the Spindle and Legends of the Loom* (N. J. Powell & Co., 1889), p. 7.
50. Ibid., p. 8.
51. B. Russell, 'The Langdale Linen Industry', p. 330.
52. Ibid., p. 331.
53. Ambleside Oral History Group, transcript of interview with Mrs Reed, 1990, p. 16. Held in Kendal Reference library.
54. B. Russell, 'The Langdale Linen Industry', p. 331.
55. Ibid.
56. Linda Parry, *Textiles of the Arts and Crafts Movement* (Thames & Hudson, 1988), pp. 71-132.
57. B. Russell, 'The Langdale Linen Industry', p. 332.
58. M. Blake, *Revival of Spinning and Weaving in Langdale*, p. 13.
59. Poem entitled 'Langdale Linen' signed and dated 'by Lizzie Pepper, February 18th 1890' cited in ibid., p. 14. as 'found in an old newspaper cutting'.
60. The address book, account and order book are kept in the Langdale archive at Cumbria Record Office, Kendal.
61. Elizabeth Longford (ed.), *Louisa, Lady in Waiting* (Jonathan Cape, 1979), p. 87. for Sandringham details.
62. Recorded conversation with the author on 2 November 1995. Mrs Reed died in March 1997.
63. Unattributed article, *The Girl's Own Paper*, p. 691.
64. In conversation 2 November 1995.
65. Ibid.
66. Ambleside Oral History Group, transcript of interview with Mrs Reed, p. 16.
67. In conversation 2 November, 1995. Harrison's of Cockermouth were themselves producers of a wide range of textiles and although there is a collection of their samples at the Victoria and Albert Museum, no archive or documentation appears to exist. If anyone has any further information the author would be very interested to learn more.
68. Ambleside Oral History Group, transcript of interview with Mrs Reed, p. 14.
69. A. Callen, *Angel in the Studio*, p. 4.

70. Author in conversation, 1995.
71. B. Russell, 'The Langdale Linen Industry', p. 332.
72. *Westmorland Gazette*, 31 March, 1923.
73. A. Fleming (ed.), *Hortus Inclusus* [Letters from John Ruskin to Susan Beever] (George Allen, 1902), p. xii.

CHAPTER FOUR

The Keswick School of Industrial Arts (including The Ruskin Linen Industry)

> The beautiful little group of silver table-ware from Keswick was a welcome departure towards finer craftsmanship, though the hammered copper bowls and ewers showed no loss of the breadth of handling demanded by Harold Stabler's bold design. This excellent artist is again responsible for some of the most satisfying decorative inventions, which the class has carried out with sincere enthusiasm and rare technical ability.[1]

The Keswick School of Industrial Arts, as shown in *The Studio* review above, made many high quality products but, as the citation also highlights, their production was dependent on a combination of technical ability and accomplished design. In this chapter I propose to explore the early history of the School by acknowledging the presence of tensions between the ideals of those who initiated its formation and others who came to teach and design there. The founders of the School, Canon Rawnsley and his wife, were undoubtedly inspired by the writings of Ruskin extolling the merits of teaching art and craft work in rural schools to alleviate unemployment. Their social and moral agenda, however, may have led them not to appreciate fully the aesthetic expertise that would contribute to the success of such an enterprise. The perception of these differences has been brought about by viewing the School's Minute Book, kept between 1884–1905, and noting Rawnsley's following comments on such matters within the same 1900 copy of *The Studio* cited above.

As a vociferous advocate of all things he believed in Canon Rawnsley was, as one of some experience, asked to contribute to a council considering the merits of a Handicraft Guild in the Newcastle area. In a meeting chaired by Earl Grey on 12 May 1900 Rawnsley was reported as stating; 'You speak of supplying designs, it is as unkind a thing as you can do. Let the village, or the workers, hammer away at their own idea or design'. As the writer of the article commented; '... one is inclined to ask whether the Keswick School of Craftwork would have come in to being if the folk with

A display of silverware made at the Keswick School of Industrial Arts.

winter leisure in that place had been left to hammer away by themselves ...'.[2] On another occasion, two years earlier, Rawnsley had written to Charles Ashbee at a time when he was considering moving his Guild from Whitechapel out to the countryside, and eventually settling on Chipping Campden. Rawnsley wrote of his belief that clean countryside air was a pre-requisite to good design, clearly implying that one would naturally be followed by the other and that 'I wish you would start your classes anywhere but in Hell'.[3]

Rawnsley's character as co-founder, with his wife, is clearly intrinsic though not lastingly fundamental to the telling of the history of the Keswick School of Industrial Arts. Before discussing its formation and relevant biographical details, however, it is perhaps interesting to note the potted history ascribed to Rawnsley by Fiona MacCarthy, biographer of some of his contemporaries.

> Canon Rawnsley (1851–1920). Vicar of Crosthwaite, near Keswick, and a Canon of Carlisle. Muscular Christian and inveterate crusader. Notoriously lacking in patience and humility. Once when returning to the Lake District, his train missed its connection. The other passengers were resigned to waiting for the next train, but not Rawnsley. He fetched the station master who immediately put a special train at his disposal. He also managed to write 37 books.[4]

Hardwicke Rawnsley, whose reputation clearly precedes him here, was a man of prodigious energy, described by John K. Walton as 'a prolific minor poet, historical novelist and topographical writer. He was also a pugnacious propagandist and campaigner on issues relating to the preservation of an idealised version of the landscape and rural society of the Lake District ...'.[5] His lasting legacy was surely secured by his role as one of the founders of the embryonic National Trust.

In the light of his disparate actions it is perhaps not surprising to learn on closer inspection that the archive records of the K.S.I.A. (as I shall now abbreviate the School) reveal Rawnsley's ideological influence; but more telling was the key role his wife Edith played in not only starting but also sustaining a day to day contribution in the running and controlling of the school.[6] On the occasions when Rawnsley was present at Committee Meetings and recorded the minutes, his erratic and largely illegible handwriting seems to endorse the somewhat impatient and irascible characteristics of his personality. While suggesting his main talent in this instance to be igniting the idea, I do not wish to totally diminish his role in the development of the School. He was uniquely placed to carve out a particular niche and make a contribution to the Arts and Crafts Movement in the Lake District because of his background, his education, his beliefs, his contacts and the use he made of his public position. For this reason the history of the K.S.I.A. has to start with Hardwicke Rawnsley.

Hardwicke Rawnsley

He was born on 28 September 1851 as one of twins to Catherine and Drummond Rawnsley, who was the vicar of Shiplake on Thames, near Henley. In this capacity his father had presided over the marriage of his long-time friend Alfred later Lord Tennyson. The family connection continued and when the poet laureate died in 1893 the pall for his coffin was designed and made by the Keswick School of Industrial Arts.

After attending Uppingham School, Rawnsley went up to Balliol College, Oxford where he encountered John Ruskin, then Slade Professor of Art. Besides becoming familiar with his writings Rawnsley was in the party of students who participated in one of Ruskin's drawing classes which included the practical element of digging Hinksey Road. As Ruskin related to his friend Henry Acland:

> My chief object is to let my pupils feel the pleasure of *useful* muscular work, and especially of the various and amusing work involved in getting a Human Pathway rightly made through a lovely country, and rightly adorned.[7]

The experiment drew attention and was ridiculed in the London papers with pictures of the 'Amateur Navvies'. Ruskin took the ridicule in good humour and accredited the technical advice to his gardener from Brantwood, 'whom he had summoned to Oxford to act as Professor of Digging'.[8] The project did, however, raise more fundamental issues concerning the appreciation and value of labour with the intention of imbuing its participants with an important lesson: 'An inch of practice is sometimes worth a yard of preaching'.[9] Central to Ruskin's beliefs was the appreciation of practical skills in not only preventing idle hands from committing evil deeds but in bringing happiness through the act of creating something. Rawnsley was to cite his professor's words later in a 1902 publication clearly identifying Ruskin as his source of inspiration and that 'his words were not forgotten':

> I would have the decoration of metal and wood brought in later, and these children as they grow shall feel the joy of adding ornament to simple surfaces of metal or wood; but always they shall be taught the use of pencil, and the delight of close observation of flower in the field and bird in the hedgerow and animal in the wild wood. We must bring joy, the joy of eye and hand-skill to our cottage homes.[10]

Rawnsley was to leave Oxford with a third class degree in Natural Sciences and seemingly little idea of a future career. His experience as a student of Ruskin, as well as the influence of Edward Thring, another Ruskin follower, at Uppingham School had, however, left him with a keen desire to do something worthwhile with his life. Initially he worked as an assistant and lay chaplain in a hostel for the homeless in Soho and it was while living and working there that he came into contact with Octavia Hill. Later she was to play a significant role in the foundation of the National Trust.

From London he moved to Bristol to work in one of the first Public School missions at Clifton College. Though he was successful in this work his strong temperance views, acted upon with his customary zeal, made him very unpopular in some quarters and the need for a change became necessary.[11] He was indeed fortunate that a small living worth £100 per annum, in the gift of some cousins from Wray, became vacant and provided him with an escape route. In December 1877 he was ordained in a ceremony at Carlisle Cathedral and took charge of the small church of St Margaret's. Whilst living in the parish of Wray he spent more time with his cousins, particularly their daughter Edith Fletcher whom he married in 1878.

Wray, close to Windermere, attracted many summer visitors including the twelve year old Beatrix Potter, whose father often rented Wray Castle. Both father and daughter were seemingly enamoured with the young priest, Mr Potter because of Rawnsley's knowledge of the Lakes and its poets and, as reported by one of her biographers;

> To Beatrix he was even more appealing, for in the warmth of his physical and mental vigour, which was prodigious, her shyness melted, and she made the stimulating discovery that it was possible for grown-up people to have enthusiasms.[12]

Her later allegiance to the Lake District and indeed the legacy of land and property she was to bequeath to the National Trust says something about this early encounter in Wray.

As the vicar of Wray, Rawnsley was now in a position to put into practice some of the ideas conveyed by Ruskin, with the emphasis very much on religious deeds. As he recorded in 1902:

> Why don't the bishops admonish their clergy to see to it that side by side with the parish church and parish room there shall be a parish workshop, where the blacksmith and the village carpenter shall of a winter evening teach all the children who will be diligent and will learn, the nature of iron and wood, and the use of their eyes and hands.[13]

The evening classes that Rawnsley and his wife, a talented water colourist, started in Wray proved popular and, finding that others in Grasmere and Ambleside were also interested, it was decided to seek some expert teaching. As Rawnsley wrote, 'To make a long story short, a lady was engaged to come down from South Kensington to give a course of lessons in the three villages, and our humble home industry in the lake district was set on foot'.[14]

It seems likely that this refers to the School of Art Woodcarving that was established in Somerset Street, South Kensington, in 1879 by the Society of Arts with the Florentine artist, Signor Bulletti as instructor. As Anthea Callen has described, 'The school was open to amateurs as well as to students taking professional training, and in the late eighties the carving of wood became a popular as well as society hobby'.[15] The blurring between amateur and professional, which is present here, provided women with the opportunity of finding 'suitable work' within the art world without being perceived as obviously needing to earn money.[16] This was also the case for the Royal School of Needlework, which similarly had a remit to undertake commercial commissions. Practical crafts like embroidery and woodcarving were deemed to be suitable female occupations and women were encouraged to train as teachers of these subjects. After three or four years they were then able to travel to venues around the country and to earn between £1 – £5 a week. One woman to follow such a path was May Watts, wife of the painter G. F. Watts

The carved wooden cover of a photograph album in the archive held at Carlisle Record Office.

who was a friend of Rawnsley and had connections with K.S.I.A. However, in the absence of any real records for this period the identity of the teachers involved remains a matter of speculation.

Before they left Wray, Edith Rawnsley expanded the curriculum in the winter evenings to include experimenting with metal repoussé. This technique, where a thin piece of metal is hammered through from the underside to make a raised pattern on the top side, was taught with the help of her mother's Swiss butler. As Rawnsley recorded 'I like to think of this man's experiment as part of the seed from which our Keswick School of Industrial Arts sprang'.[17]

Crosthwaite; from Parish Rooms to Permanent Building

In 1883 Rawnsley was given a larger parish when he became the vicar of St Kentigern in Crosthwaite, near Keswick. Reluctantly forsaking the proximity of his old professor at Brantwood, Rawnsley saw again the opportunity of putting Ruskin's ideas into practice. He wrote '… we were amongst a people who must necessarily have little work to do out of the tourist season, and were in a town which had none of the excitement of the "threepenny theatre" or "penny-gaff" to act as counter attraction'.[18] In the winter of 1883–1884 a large committee of interested parties was formed including 'a gentleman in the neighbourhood who was an artist and designer'.[19] Although un-named in the account by Rawnsley, his identity would appear to be R. W. Oddie as further use of his designs was mentioned when the Minute Book came into use for the following winter session in 1884. Again a teacher was engaged from South Kensington and woodcarving together with brass repoussé work, under the tuition of Mrs Rawnsley and a local jeweller, were taught on three nights in the Parish Rooms. It would appear that woodcarving classes were also held during the day for 'the ladies of the neighbourhood' when a fee was charged so that, as Rawnsley stated, it 'enabled us to hold a class free of charge for working-men and lads during the evening'.[20]

Within a month pupils in the metal class were producing simple brass and copper plates for doors, which were later sold. In all the first five-month session incurred expenses of £181 but this was offset with the sale of products which totalled some £118. Costs were kept low by using the Parish Rooms, for which no charge was made, but it did mean that after every session benches and tools had to be cleared away to allow for normal parochial use the following day. The need for greater accountability as the enterprise increased was reflected not only by the Committee Minute Book but also by the posting of 'Rules' for the session from 1 November 1884 until March 1885. They read:

1. No persons under 16 years of age will be admitted as members.
2. The Committee reserve to themselves the right to discontinue instruction to any member of the School who does not show sufficient aptitude or carefulness in the work.
3. Tools, materials etc., will be provided by the Committee, and all articles worked by members of the school will be the property of the Committee, who pay the workers for all articles they consider to have a marketable value.
4. No work will be allowed to be done in connection with the School except from designs approved by the Committee.
5. Amateurs joining the School will pay for their tools and materials and 2*s.* 6*d.* for each lesson. They will not necessarily be paid for the articles they produce, but may retain them or sell them to the Committee, according to arrangement. Amateurs who, after receiving lessons, wish to continue their connection with the school may do so by subscribing 10*s.* 6*d.* for each winter season. They will also adhere to Rule 4.
6. Lessons will be given and working meetings held in the Parish Room, when possible, on Tuesday, Thursday, and Saturday evenings, from 7 to 9.30. Amateur class for lessons and working on Saturday mornings from 10 to 12.[21]

Besides the set of rules, a committee of fifteen, including Rev. and Mrs Rawnsley, together with a treasurer, Mr Edwin Jackson and a secretary, Rev. J. S. Ostle appended their names to the aims of the School. This read:

> Keswick School of Industrial Arts
>
> The aim of this School is to find remunerative employment for working men and others, in spare hours, or when out of work, by teaching them such art industries as can be profitably carried out in their own homes.
>
> The Art Industries taught will be brass and other metal work, carving, embroidery, etc.
>
> One of the chief objects of the promoters will be to secure the conformity of all designs to the finest examples of various styles of work at the best periods.
>
> It is hoped that the School will eventually be self-supporting, the cost of the materials, tools, production, heating and lighting of work-room, etc., being covered by the sale of articles through local tradesmen, and the execution of orders.
>
> The articles produced in brass and other metals will be wall-sconces, plaques, trays, lamps, mantelpiece furniture, finger plates, blowers for fireplaces, caskets, bowls, silver ornaments, etc.
>
> All wood carving will be from the solid, in low relief, and suitable for furniture. No fretwork will be allowed.
>
> The School will also provide designs for needlework, and a small assortment of materials suitable for carrying them out.
>
> The promoters wish to direct special attention to the differences there will be in character between the ordinary manufactured articles in brass and other materials, and those produced entirely by hand in the manner of old work, and under strict personal supervision. They hope for assistance from all who are interested in the revival of industrial arts, and in the effort to bring the designer into more immediate relation with the workman until they become more or less identified, as was the case at all periods when the arts were truly living.[22]

The last sentence in its reference to 'when the arts were truly living' reflected the Rawnsleys endorsement of Ruskin's words and the essence of his influential essay, 'The Nature of Gothic' (1853). However, it also underlines the fundamental problem for many associated with the Arts and Crafts Movement. In order to sell the individual work of a craftsman at a price acceptable to the market place it had to be, both in terms of design and skill, of a very high quality and that level of speciality was rarely found naturally within one being. As Ruskin wrote:

> You must either make a tool of the creature, or a man of him. You cannot make both. Men were not intended to work with the accuracy of tools, to be precise and perfect in all their actions. If you will have that precision out of them, and make their fingers measure degrees like cog-wheels, and their arms strike curves like compasses, you must inhumanize them.[23]

To encourage men on a road of self-discovery, and to express their creativity through this into a piece of art or craft work, did not necessarily lead to a product that could realistically be sold in a competitive commercial market. Similarly to espouse the workmanship of medieval stonemasons only in terms of their individually carved gargoyles is to underestimate the accuracy, discipline and precision required of their creative skills when dictated to by the architect in his brief to create a lasting building. The business of making the K.S.I.A. self-sufficient required attention to the realities of the more sophisticated commercial late-Victorian market place, rather than any idealised notion of medieval patronage. These realities included acknowledging the effects of foreign competition. It is perhaps not surprising that in outlining the initial objectives of the School Rawnsley had, like Ruskin and Fleming, not only espoused the merits of individual craft work but had also criticised the results of a laissez-faire trade policy which resulted in cheap imports. Consequently one aim of the School had been:

A fine example of repoussé work (unattributed) made at Keswick.

> To show that there was here in England, while we are crying out that German cheap art labour or Japanese cheap art labour is ruining us, an abundance of skill of hand which is wasted, but which, if any education worth its name could be given to the whole working man – to his eye, to his hand, to his heart as well as his head – could and would help England here and now.[24]

It is, however, at this stage when the practical realities began to impinge on the ideals that the reader may perceive that, while Rawnsley may have 'never missed an opportunity of making the work of the school known', he was also busy with other projects.[25] He was to play a vociferous role as 'watchdog of the Lakes' and was an active member of many associations including the Lake District Defence Society (as was the founder of the Langdale Linen Industry, Albert Fleming) which was formed in 1883. In 1888 Rawnsley stood successfully for the Cumberland County Council as an Independent Liberal, a position he held for twelve years . These and other numerous commitments together with his writing and extended trips abroad meant, as has been observed that, 'The detailed work of the parish was conducted mainly through curates'.[26] Fortunately the appointment of a Committee, who met on a fortnightly basis, and some key personnel ensured the continuity needed in the day to day running of the School but they still deferred to the Rawnsleys when it came to important decisions.

In November 1884, a telegram was sent to Mrs Rawnsley in London, requesting the appointment of an experienced teacher to take up a position in the new year of 1885. In the 'Minutes' of 24 January 1885, Mr Oddie also made reference to another key member of the School and recommended 'that in future Miss Elliot's remuneration be 9/- a week instead of 6/-'. This was agreed unanimously. Miss Elliot played a central role in the School by securing orders from customers and tourists during the summer months from her home at Slack House on Main Street, and these were fulfilled later in the year, when the School re-opened in the October. The 'Minutes' of 3 October report that '£55 worth of goods have been sold, leaving a deficit of £5.8.5*d.* Assets to the value of £66'. Getting the books to balance was becoming more difficult and Dr. Knight proposed that 'no one in the school should be paid for any work done, until the work was sold'.[27] This followed on from an earlier decision when it was

A prie-dieu with inlaid repoussé work.

A wall cabinet with inlaid repoussé work.

decided that only those *out* of regular employment should be paid immediately. The exception then being if the work had been sold straight away.

A press cutting, from an unattributed newspaper but dated 17 April 1886, reflected the Committee's desire to broaden the market for the School's products by participating in London exhibitions. This was made possible through the Arts and Crafts Exhibition Society and the School's affiliation to the Home Arts and Industries Association, which it joined in November 1884. The cutting also reveals the presence then of some thirty members who 'vary in age from 15 to 50' and the School's aim that 'eventually every article produced may be the handiwork of one man from beginning to end'. It was hoped that crafts other than hammered metal work and woodcarving would be taught in the future. Meanwhile; 'Every article made in the school is stamped with the school mark, and nothing is allowed to be sold by individual members'. The newspaper article, which also included itemised accounts, concluded by stating.

> The result of the past year's working show the school to be self-supporting; and that it is in no little measure due to the interest which Mrs Rawnsley and her too small band of helpers have shown in it.[28]

For the second winter session a wood carving teacher from Carlisle was engaged for the sum of £9. In order to pay him a special collection was made within the neighbourhood. This, according to Rawnsley, was the only time such action was necessary. It seems likely that this employee was Mr Little of Lowther Street in Carlisle. The *Carlisle Journal*, in reviewing a later exhibition, reported 'The examples of wood carving … are not numerous but they are sufficient to show that the pupils have made much progress under their teacher, Mr Little …'.[29] So successful did the School become in attracting pupils, it was decided that a form of selection should be invoked whereby 'no lad should be admitted to work till he could prove by attendance at the drawing class his ability to trace his pattern for himself on to the metal or wood'.[30]

The scope and extent of the metal work was also increased when the School set up its own 'iron-room', adjacent to the Parish Rooms, complete with concrete flooring, blow-pipes, anvil and vices. One of the best students undertook the responsibility of teaching himself and then passing on his new knowledge to others as he progressed. Expenditures had doubled by the end of the third session but so had their sales, indicating a profit of £131. An exhibition held in the local Town Hall, as Rawnsley recalled, was met with 'astonishment on the faces of some of the townsmen who found that this work had been done in their midst by men and lads whom they knew well enough in any capacity but that of wood or metal-worker'.[31]

As the enterprise grew issues relating to further appointments, such as Mr Highton as the drawing master in 1 November 1887, and concerns that the members should buy their own tools, or at least undertake to purchase them from money earned, were raised. The discussion on the issue of prize money resulted in a decision that the School should receive the prize and that the individual worker be allocated one third of the money. By these means, together with the sale of goods, the School's income for 1888 had risen to £534 2*s.* 11*d.* and the demands for a more permanent workshop were beginning to be raised.

So far this account has reflected the concerns over male unemployment, resulting from some form of incapacity or seasonal fluctuation in the demand for their services in the Keswick area, and what the School could do for them. At the same time the School also complied with Rawnsley's somewhat dichotomous stance which sought to both protect and promote the traditional skills and attractions of the Lake District. As J. K. Walton stated; 'His campaigns against development sought to protect idealised rural virtue against the contagion of urban vice, providing him with a congenial way of justifying his existence by offering "uplift" to selected members of the urban [and rural] working class …'.[32]

In this next section, before discussing what was to become the next phase of the School, I want to look at another aspect of the K.S.I.A. and its contribution to what became known as the Ruskin Linen Industry. As early as 1887 some reference was made in a Committee meeting to contact with the Kensington School of Art Needlework in connection with displaying some 'coffin work'. Unfortunately, Rawnsley's 'Minute' notes are largely indecipherable so whether this is in reference to some pall work undertaken by the women of Keswick is not clear. The first real advancement in discussing a linen industry appeared in a special meeting held on 30 April 1889, with an advancement of some £50 being made for that purpose. This, as becomes evident, developed alongside and then separately from the later activities of the School.

The Linen Industry at Keswick

As discussed in chapter three on the Langdale Linen Industry, and elsewhere, the two key figures to initiate the revival of this industry in the Lake District were Albert Fleming and Marion Twelves.[33] As the main practitioner and manager at Elterwater it is not known exactly why Twelves chose to move her work to the School in Keswick. Rawnsley's comments suggest her motives were idealistic; '... she had seen enough of the pleasure brought into cottage homes by the humming wheel, to make her determined to do for Cumberland what she had done for Westmorland ...'.[34] However, an account Twelves published in an American magazine suggests her motives might relate more to a greater appreciation and control over her own individual work as a craftswoman. She wrote:

> In 1889, I took my work to Keswick in the hope of obtaining more independence and reliable support in carrying out what I considered (and still consider) to be Mr Ruskin's economic principles, and to obtain a wider influence for the work ...[35]

Her conviction as a true disciple of Ruskin's teachings, as previously mentioned when describing her work at Langdale, was made clear by her reference to *Fors Clavigera*, the letters to workmen and labourers of Great Britain, when she had cited letter 93 and written; '... you come forward to be givers, not receivers in this human world – that you *give* your time, your thoughts, your labour, and the reward of your labour as far as you can spare it, for the help of the poor and needy'.[36] Guarded affirmation of his influence on her work had been forthcoming in a personal letter where Ruskin had revealed to Twelves; 'It is terribly difficult for me to understand how the more or less visionary talk of my books can be of use to a mind so cheerfully and practically strong as yours – but I am nevertheless delighted in my wonderment that it is so'.[37]

Ruskin's name in association with a linen industry was, according to Twelves, not given until the occasion of his seventy fifth birthday in 1894. At this time she wrote;

> Mr Ruskin signed an authority for me to use his name and his motto 'Today' as a Trade Mark ... and I may here set down once and for

> all that my industry is the *only one* [sic] of any description having authority from Mr Ruskin to use his name, and that no other industry in the Lake District or elsewhere … except a class of Greek Lace Workers in Coniston village …[38]

Confusion over the attribution of this title seemingly begins here. Despite Twelves' statement, the very first point of the terms of agreement, which were drawn up with the K.S.I.A. in June 1889, read: 'The *Ruskin Linen Industry* is started in Keswick as a branch of *the Keswick School of Industrial Arts*'. It continued:

2. Miss Twelves undertakes the management of the Linen Industry, without salary for the first six months, & subject to further arrangement. Salary not [to] exceed £1 a week.
3. An account of all bills and payments for work in connection with the Linen Industry to be rendered *monthly* to the Treasurer of K.S.I.A.
4. No expenses to be incurred without authority from the Executive Committee.
5. No letters to be written to the public press relating to the Keswick School without authority of Executive Committee. Such letters to appear under the … names of Mrs Rawnsley & Miss Twelves.
6. Keswick to be Miss Twelves' headquarters & residence.
7. Agreement with Miss Twelves to continue subject to notice of six months on either side.
8. It is understood that the name "Ruskin Linen Industry" is attached to Miss Twelves' work wherever it may be carried out.[39]

While the last point does indicate her personal affiliation with Ruskin, this does seem quite a restrictive agreement considering that her reasons for moving were given as a need for more independence. Although it is hand-written on the headed notepaper of the School it was, however, unsigned.

The teaching of hand spinning and weaving was to be undertaken from 'St Kentigern's', a building on the Penrith Road and originally one of the first woollen mills in the region. The 'Minutes' of an early meeting appeared in the Crosthwaite Church Parish magazine setting out its aims and that:

> The thread will be spun by women in their own homes, and the linen cloth woven by a weaver on the premises … the matter has been taken up with the sole object of benefiting the workers … all who have wheels in their possession, and will lend or sell them, will be favouring a good object.[40]

This reflected a similarity to the practice in the Langdales where

Twelves had worked previously. The £50 was invested in equipment which included a loom, twelve spinning wheels costing 12/6 each, a warping mill, learner's flax, a mangle and two bobbins. Later in December 1889 the accounts recorded that £124 10*s.* 9*d.* was received for the Spinning Industry and that £23 2*s.* 6*d.* had been paid into the bank. The 'Minutes' of a meeting held on 29 November 1889 noted that; '... [the] Committee heard Miss Twelves report of the Linen Industry and decided that a weaver should be engaged for three months and that a meeting of the Committee should be called in three months time to hear a future report'. They also recorded; 'A cordial vote of thanks to Miss Twelves for her kindness in establishing the industry and of confidence in her good management'.[41]

At this stage all seemed well with the industry as it secured enough orders for the natural coloured hand-spun and woven cloth to keep its spinners occupied throughout the winter months. The first public and social gathering for the group of spinners was held in the Parish Room on 17 February 1890 with 'the spinners in their neat caps and aprons spinning away in a semi-circle'.[42] The name of the first weaver to be appointed was not recorded but on 21 April 1890 the 'Minutes' show that his work had proved unsatisfactory and he was replaced by Robert Shearman. Despite the fact that his work was also recorded as not meeting the standards laid down by Miss Twelves, herself an accomplished weaver, he was nevertheless named in 1900 as the weaver of Ruskin's pall. Subsequent arrangements also show that weaving was undertaken through the occasional visits of Mr Philips from Cockermouth. Following an exhibition of their wares at Keswick the industry moved on to the national stage. Of the exhibits that appeared that year at The Armourers and Braziers' exhibition in London in May, the Home Arts Industries exhibition in Birmingham

Marion Twelves spinning outside St. George's Cottage in Crosthwaite, Keswick. From the Abigail Reed Archive and kindly supplied by John Marsh.

in June, the Arts and Crafts Society Exhibition in London, in October, one might deduce that these consisted of Marion Twelves' own weavings.

Much of the other linen produced was sold to be used for embroidery and it seems that this craft was also being taught at Keswick alongside finer cut-linen work based on reticella, the lace work produced traditionally in Italy and Greece. John Ruskin's enthusiasm for this work, shown to best effect when contrasted against a dark red or blue silk background, led to it also being known as Ruskin Lace as well as Greek Lace.[43] This technique, which involved cutting into the linen and in-filling with stitching in a decorative pattern and darning the edges to avoid fraying, was also part of the industries at Langdale and Bowness. At Keswick it was applied together with embroidery in the production of bedspreads, cushions, sideboard cloths, antimacassars and other domestic linen. In 1890 the largest proportion of the linen industry wage account, £48 13*s.* 11½*d.*, was allocated for embroidery.[44]

A year later experiments were carried out to dye the linen, so increasing the range on offer, with orders for terracotta, orange and purple being recorded. The progress of the industry was not without mishap, however, and bad workmanship by an inexperienced member in 1891 was recorded as costing them £20. This would have been off-set against the accruing stock, where linen was priced at five shillings a yard.[45] Recognition of their increasing expertise was demonstrated clearly a year later with the commission to produce, within three days, the pall to cover Tennyson's coffin as it journeyed to Westminster Abbey.

> On a piece of unbleached linen was embroidered to a design of Mrs Edith Rawnsley forty two blossoms of the wild rose of England, worked in natural colours, to tally with his years as Poet Laureate. The Pall was taken to his home at Aldworth in Sussex to be placed in position before the coffin was transferred by carriage and train to London.[46]

Tennyson's son, Hallam, wrote to the family friend Hardwicke Rawnsley to record his thanks for 'this beautiful gift, wrought by their loving hands, which he would have valued so highly and which will always be to us a treasured possession'.[47] Unlike the pall made eight years later for Ruskin and kept at Coniston Museum, the whereabouts of this historic piece of textile work are no longer known.

The success of the spinning, weaving and embroidery, some seven hundred pieces of work produced in one year, which included their first Communion Cloth for St Mary Abbot's in Kensington, was marred by the increasing differences between Twelves and the Committee of the K.S.I.A., particularly Mrs Rawnsley. Again these seem to be centred around Twelves' concerns about individual effort and control. Following a strongly worded letter on the failure to recognise her total commitment to the work and to consult her on exhibitions where her work was to be shown, Marion Twelves handed in her resignation. As required she served the Committee with six months' notice and voiced her intentions to carry on the linen work 'on her own account'. The 'Minutes' of 5 February 1894 recorded that 'The Committee saw no choice left them but to accept your resignation but require time for a decision on the further steps to be taken'.[48] The discussions as to the terms of this severance, with the Committee threatening to seize items of machinery and stock if Twelves did not accept their offer, had come to a head against the background of the building and opening of the new permanent School premises in Lake Road.

After two months Dr. Douglas and Mr Anderson, who were acting on Twelves' behalf, presented three different proposals to the Committee which involved sums of money varying from £100 – £150 to buy the plant at 'St Kentigern's'. Also under consideration were issues concerning embroidery, which had not been mentioned in the original agreement, whereby the K.S.I.A. was asked not to compete for a period of a year. At this point Mrs Rawnsley intervened with a conciliatory offer which acknowledged 'the valuable and gratuitous services of Miss Twelves' by reducing the sum required to £80. On 9 April 1894 Twelves agreed to sign and pay '£45 for the plant for making Home-Spun and Hand Made Linen. £25 to be paid on the date of signing and £20 on or before July 31st 1894'. Financial links appeared to be severed finally in a meeting held in November 1895 whereby it was 'resolved that the balance due to the Treasurer on the Linen Industry be written off from the main school account'. It was also agreed that certain items should be accredited to the Linen Industry, these included a present to Professor Ruskin for £5, the Tennyson pall for £4 7*s.* and expenses regarding a County Council grant for £12 9*s.* 6*d.*[49]

Marion Twelves left her base at 'St Kentigern's' and moved into two cottages on High Hill where she continued to work for the next thirty years. The cottages carried the sign of 'The Ruskin Linen Industry' and were known as 'St George's Cottages' indicating their allegiance to the Guild of St George.[50] A loan of £25 'minuted' on 3 February 1898, with the condition that it was to be repaid within six months (which it was) did, however, indicate a continued level of co-operation between the Ruskin Linen Industry and the K.S.I.A. This state of truce was made most apparent in the making of the pall that covered Ruskin's coffin in 1900. To cite Benjamin's comprehensive description:

> It is a natural-coloured linen, lined and bordered with deep rose silk, and beautifully embroidered with scattered wild roses, sprays of leaves and buds interspersed with fallen petals. In the centre is a wreath of wild roses, the emblem of St George, encircling the initials 'J. R.' and 'Unto this last', the title of one of his books. This fine example of needlework, 7ft. 6ins by 6ft. 8ins., was designed by Mrs. E. Rawnsley, drawn by Mr. Harold Stabler, and the wreath embroidered by Miss Douglas. The other ladies of Keswick who had a part in this lovely work of art were: Miss Norris, Mrs. Taylor, Mrs. Hooper, Miss E. G. Newby, Mrs. Grant, Miss Swain, and Miss Ethel Broatch, all under the supervision of Marion Twelves. The thread for the linen was spun by Mrs. Youdale, and woven by Robert Shearman. It was put on exhibition at the Royal Albert Hall in the same year.[51]

Two years later, in a publication dedicated to Marion Twelves; 'A devoted friend and Disciple of John Ruskin ...', Rawnsley referred to the solace she gained from the thought 'that at least the pall that lay upon the Master's coffin was handspun and handwoven here at Keswick under her own direction'.[52]

In the meantime the linen industry progressed, exhibiting and winning many prizes. Royal and aristocratic patronage was an important element in promoting this work as were the commissions gained with the upsurge of Church decoration throughout and beyond the nineteenth century. In 1901 a review of the Home Arts and Industries Association stated:

> The Ruskin Linen Industry of Keswick has made great advance this year. Over fifty varieties of linen have been made, and work has been purchased and highly commended by H.R.H. Princess Louise, the Marchioness of Lorne, H.R.H. the Duchess of Albany, Lady Muncaster, and others. The Pall used at the funeral of the late Bishop of Carlisle was made by the Ruskin Linen Industry, which also supplied the 'fine cloth' for Holy Communion to two churches.[53]

However, while they had been united in honouring Ruskin, some animosity remained. Such matters were seemingly exacerbated by the 'strong characters of the individual teachers'.[54] As Marion Twelves indicated these differences centred around issues of her professional commitment and the essentially amateur volunteers who, because of their membership of the management committee, were perceived to have more control in decision-making than she did. The issue of who managed this linen industry was resolved when Twelves ended the working affiliation with the School, and the Ruskin

Linen Industry was formally incorporated into the Guild of St George on 6 September. This may have brought a more consistent form of financial support and independence for Marion Twelves but it also meant that she had to spend more of her time with correspondence, teaching, addressing meetings and publicising the industry.

In 1907 the responsibility of running the industry was shared between Twelves and Ada Hooper, as it continued to attract customers and pupils on a national and international basis. When Marion Twelves retired in 1917, Ada Hooper took full responsibility, undertaking to pay the rent on the two cottages and supply a yearly report and balance sheet to the Guild. In return they sent a sub-committee to visit once a year and maintained the right to withdraw Ruskin's name if they were not satisfied with the industry's progress. Although the Guild did not sell the cottages until 1962 the work, as with all craft industries, was badly affected by the First World War. While the production of linen may have ceased to be viable, interest in the making of Greek and Ruskin Lace continued and is still taught today with a teaching lineage that can be traced back to Marion Twelves who died in 1929 at the age of eighty six. She had taught Mrs Coward, who taught Mrs Raby who in turn taught Elizabeth Prickett, which has meant the fine art of lace making has continued in the Lake District.

The K.S.I.A. in Lake Road

The twelve months between 1893 to 1894 constituted a watershed for the K.S.I.A. Not only was the linen industry established; this period also saw the building of a permanent School ensuring further commitment to an art and craft industry in Keswick.

After working in the Parish Rooms for ten years, plans to finance a larger and permanent residence for the School became a reality. As early as 1889 an appeal had been launched to raise the £1500 needed to acquire a new site with enough money to build workshops, a showroom and an office. To this end classes, usually only held during the winter months, were run throughout the year, increasing the numbers attending to around one hundred. Money raised from the sale of the work produced in 1888 was estimated at £1,000, which served to prove that not only was the School self-sufficient but it was also able to contribute to the economy of the town. This enhanced the Committee's argument for a permanent building, which, with the added provision of more skilled teachers, would further the working opportunities for the inhabitants of Keswick. An article, in the *Carlisle Journal* on 22 May 1891, praised the quality of the woodcarving but at the same time indicated the growing

The Keswick School of Industrial Arts in Lake Road which was officially opened by Lady Muncaster in 1894.

importance of metalwork, which was fast becoming the major product of the School, with designs that were inspired by multicultural and international sources.

> The copper and brass work seems to command the attention of most of the sixty workers at the school who devote their leisure or, as in some cases, in which men who have been incapacitated for their regular employment, the whole of the working day to hammering and carving. An altar cross done in copper and gilding metal is a conspicuous object at one end of the room … A copper sconce … contains a reminiscence of the Vatican, two lions with tails and wings florescent, the centre being filled with a conventional cypress. Two dishes … are of a decidedly Oriental stamp. They are copies of dishes from a Buddhist temple in Ceylon used for the purpose of offering fruit and flowers to Buddha …

The article continued with more examples of the work and workers including 'John Tolsen, formerly a platelayer and now a cripple' who had made two tea-trays, 'one of the Indian sacred heart design, and the other reminding one of the peony'. Arabian and Rhodian influences were also mentioned, the latter in connection with 'an electro type copy' of a design from South Kensington Museum. The

Work on display in the school.

versatility of individual members was also demonstrated through the work of John Fisher Banks, who had produced a communion service book binding with a thirteenth century design, 'the original of which, it is believed, is in ivory at Ravenna', as well as hammering out a 'jewelled cross'.[55]

On 3 May 1893, in his capacity as Chairman, Rawnsley with every confidence in securing the School's future signed a contract for the new building. Funds had been raised in various ways; £300 had come from the School's income, £200 was given by the County Council and £800 was donated by friends and supporters through public subscription. With advice from friends including Holman Hunt, Walter Crane and G. F. Watts the new building for the School was designed by Paley and Austen of Lancaster. In producing a plan they complied with the Committee, and their advisers, and 'faithfully carried out their wishes to have an unpretentious building which should be in accord with the Old Lake Country style of domestic architecture and should have sufficient character to render it an ornament to the main approach'.[56] Later that year the much travelled Rawnsley was able to pause in his carriage on the way to Switzerland and lay the foundation stone. The School was opened officially in 1894 by Lady Muncaster. Ruskin's portrait was given a prominent position and some words of Browning were replicated on the front façade of the building. They read

> The Loving Eye and Patient Hand
> Shall work with Joy and Bless the Land.

The itemised cost of building the School which had utilised 'local materials, slate and stone, and incorporated a spinning gallery, a feature of local vernacular architecture . . .',[57] was recorded as follows:

	£	s.	d.
Builder	711	9	6
Joiner	290	12	9
Plumber	59	16	1
Painter	50	0	0
Making Road	23	15	11
Gates	20	0	0
Hedge	15	0	0
Garden	9	7	0
[illegible] for drying	4	0	0
Architect	65	0	0
Total	1249	1	3
Furnishings (approximate)	198	13	2[58]

As always, aware of the importance of the tourist trade to their market, Rawnsley had pre-empted the event by submitting an entry to *Jenkinson's Practical Guide to the English Lakes* (1893). It read;

> The next place to be visited on the way up the street is the Keswick School of Industrial Arts ... which now gives employment to more than one hundred members during the winter evenings. They do metal repoussé work – silver, copper, and brass – and wood carving.

With a permanent building and better working conditions the School was now in a position to improve its own design facilities. 'South Kensington Dept.' was consulted on workshop provision and the recommendation of an art teacher. Following negotiations Miss C. Masters, who lived in Penrith and held a certificate of training, expressed her willingness to teach at Keswick. An offer of help from a Miss Yates was also accepted. It seems clear that there was quite a fluid throughput of female teaching staff at the School with varying degrees of effectiveness. The 'Minutes' also reveal discussions on the fees paid by student carvers whereby it was agreed that 1/6 of their 2/6 charge should be returned to them if they were a regular attender during the winter months. It was stipulated, however, that all fees had to be paid before the work was given out. At this time the School was also in negotiation with 'Mr Purdon Clark' with regard to making copies, in wood and metal, of items on loan from the collections held at South Kensington Museum. Further discussions relating to Mrs Rawnsley's expenses when selecting 'specimens of art work from South Kensington to form the promised loan collection for the Fitzpark Museum' illustrate the derivative nature of the designs employed for much of the work produced at the School when a resident designer was not employed.[59]

In 1896 Rawnsley engaged Arthur W. Simpson to teach woodcarving, paying him 27/6*d.* per lesson. This was to be a shared teaching commitment with his young assistant Harold Stabler, who taught on alternate Tuesdays.[60] Stabler had spent his time in Kendal, not only as an apprentice woodcarver with the Simpson's firm but also in acquiring a teaching certificate and developing his notable artistic skills as a designer at the Art School. In 1898 he was awarded the silver medal by Lady Bentinck as the best art student of the year.[61] In April, of the same year, Stabler was approached by the Keswick School of Industrial Arts to become their first full-time teacher. Following an interview with the Committee on Saturday 9 July, when his designs were inspected, it was decided to engage him for one year from October 1898 at a salary of £110 per year.

A carved chair designed by Harold Stabler.

A letter which Stabler addressed to Mrs Rawnsley, the following July, however, illustrated not only his feelings of growing disquiet about the standard of some members' work but also the way in which he had to defer to the Rawnsleys' authority. Although clearly involved with the day to day practicalities of running the School the question of remuneration was not within his remit. This, as he implied, led some members to exploit the situation and for Stabler to request that 'perhaps you could speak to them plainly about these extravagant wages'. Stabler goes on to single out a man called 'Clarks' for particular attention who, in listing ten items, which included mowing the School lawn, for payment in one week, had claimed the sum of £1 17*s.* 0*d.* As the head teacher, with increased responsibility, Stabler was paid only slightly more and argued that in his claim Clarks, 'a man of no special ability, no special training ...' was guilty of 'a great imposition'.[62]

Despite this expression of dissatisfaction, compounded by further correspondence relating discussions on the amount of teaching undertaken and the familiar problem of time spent on his own work, Stabler's influence on the quality of the designs and skills of the School became apparent almost immediately. He was clearly able to interpret his designs into more than one medium, moving from wood to metal work. In this as Tanya Harrod was to observe of his later work; 'Stabler's versatility sets him apart from most silversmiths ...'.[63] Of the pieces he designed at Keswick, which were accepted for the Arts and Crafts Society Exhibition in 1899, was

A desk inlaid with metal repoussé work, the carved hearts and pomegranates echo influences from Voysey and art nouveau.

a brass jug made by Thomas Spark and two copper bowls, one executed by Henry Towers and the other by Robert Temple. The presence of one of the School's outside contributing designers, Llewellyn Rathbone, however, was to be a catalyst for Stabler resulting in his letter of resignation in March 1900. This the Committee 'accepted with great regret and ... expressed their gratitude to him and their high appreciation of his services to the school with their best wishes for his future career'.[64] Stabler was to work with Rathbone, firstly in Liverpool and subsequently at the Sir John Cass Technical Institute in London, before moving on to work at the Royal School of Art from 1912–1926. Stabler's work is perhaps best remembered today in collaboration with his wife Phoebe, and the Poole Pottery.[65]

The K.S.I.A. published receipts and expenditures for the year beginning October 1898 which show an exact balancing of receipts and payments, with £643 9*s.* 9½*d.* being paid to the workers, £48 15*s.* to Miss Elliot, £21 5*s.* to Miss Norris and £119 3*s.* 4*d.* to Mr. Stabler. Subscription to the Home Arts Industries was £5 12*s.* 6*d.* and gas and coal cost £14 19*s.* 3*d.* Mr Rathbone was paid £2 1*s.* 3*d.* for his sample of work. From goods sold they received £1,439 0*s.* 8*d.* Materials and tools raised £14 10*s.* 3½*d.* and subscriptions and fees brought in £7 3*s.* 0*d.* In total their assets were valued at £1,467 9*s.* 4*d.* with £259 16*s.* 0*d.* held in a reserve fund.

Harold Stabler's successor was to be Herbert J. Maryon who was granted the title of 'Director' of School and deemed to be '... responsible for its working, subject only to the authority of the committee' for the salary of £110 per annum.[66] Two other appointments were also made, firstly 'a first-rate teacher of drawing and design' presumably to replace Miss Norris. Recommendations were made by Walter Crane and in July 1900 Miss Collinson was appointed for the salary of £100, which it was stated would also be made up by 'outside engagements'. Secondly, following her resignation earlier in the year, it became necessary to replace Miss Elliot who had occupied a central position in the running of the School. Besides taking the orders she had, as Rawnsley described, been 'the friend and confidante of all the workers from the first, giving out or taking in the work, and paying for it its just value to the worker'.[67] The duties of the succeeding 'Saleswoman', however, following an interview with Mrs Rawnsley, were defined as follows:

> Hours of attendance 10–1, 2–5 or 7. Account to be kept of all work. Salary £1 per week, £52 per annum, with two weeks holiday.[68]

A decision was also made to award a scholarship to a child of 'bona-fide' parents, presumably where either mother or father had attended or was a member of the School. The first elected scholar, recorded on 9 February 1901, was Mary Lizzie Stanley.

In May Mrs Rawnsley reported that the evening classes during the winter had averaged around thirty and in November another new teacher and designer was appointed, this time to replace Miss Collinson. Isobel MacBean, as the photograph album of items she designed in the archive reveals, proved to be a notable talent but she too remained at the Keswick School for less than a year. When she left, it was to work in London with Kate Fisher, a student contemporary of Harold Stabler at Kendal Art School. Kate's father, Alexander Fisher, had been a national scholar at South Kensington between 1884–86 and like many art schools, Kendal also awarded scholarships for students to attend there. It was, however, as a result of his scholarship to study in Italy and France that Alexander Fisher had been able to establish an enamelling workshop at the Central School of Art. This proved an invaluable source to training aspiring jewellers, like Isabel MacBean and Kate Fisher, in a craft where fashion meant that enamelling played a significant part in the design.[69]

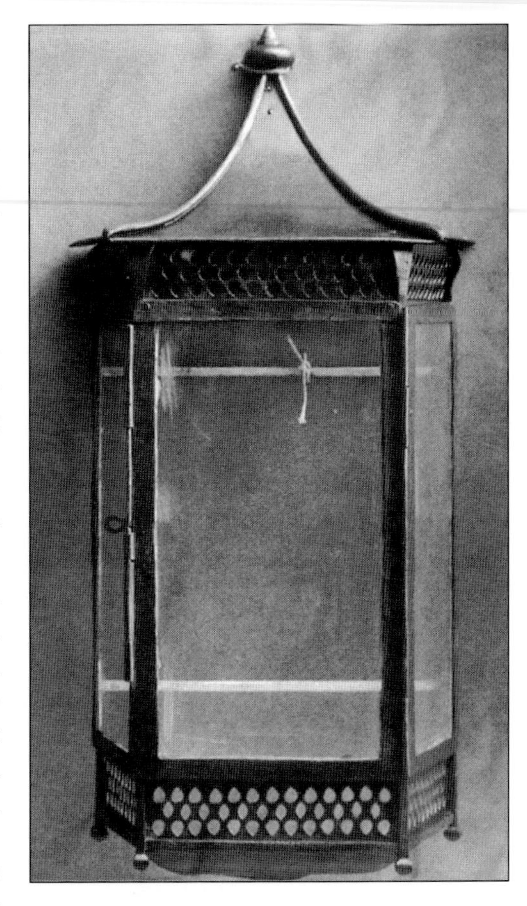

A hall lamp designed by Isobel MacBean.

Herbert Maryon, Stabler's successor, was himself a jeweller and metalworker and soon after his appointment he tried to get the

A silver and enamel casket designed for H.R.H. Princess Louise by H. J. Maryon.

Committee to increase his salary by paying him an extra 10% commission, for items sold. The commercial nature of this suggestion was not compatible with the ideology of the School and instead the Committee agreed a new rate for his overtime and made a substantial increase to his salary, raising it to £200. All however, was not well and the friction between Miss Cliffe, the Secretary and Saleswoman, and Mr Maryon resulted in her resignation. Miss MacBean had also left and was replaced by Miss Ackery. Despite the apparent concerns with personnel, a comprehensive array of metalwork was selected for the prestigious Arts and Crafts Exhibition Society in 1903 confirming the high standard of the aesthetic and technical skill that the School had achieved at this time. The catalogue described some of these items as follows:

Case of Keswick School of Industrial Arts
Designed by H. J. Maryon

a. Casket, silver & enamel lent by H.R.H. Princess Louise
b. Mermaid Ring, diamond & silver lent by Mrs. G. M. Bishop
c. Silver Cup £10 10*s.*
d. Silver Cup £10 10*s.*
e. Silver salt & spoon £2 2*s.*
f. Box, silver & enamel £2 10*s.*
g. Plated soup tureen £7 7*s.*
h. Pewter Box £1 10*s.*

In all twenty six items were listed, the last two of which were accredited as the design of Isabel MacBean. The display had been made by the eight following listed workers; J. Richardson, T. Spark, J. Clark, R. Temple, J. Spark, M. Armstrong, J. Rigg and A. Vickers.[70]

In 1902 a Benefit Club was introduced whereby, for five shillings a year, members who were paid on the basis of piecework could safeguard their income on the understanding that if they were able to work at home they would not receive sick pay. Other employment issues, however, were not so easily resolved. The 'Minutes' record the problems that both staff and members were having in working with the Director, Maryon, whose salary the Committee had nevertheless agreed to raise in 1903 to £225. More staff resignations followed and despite previous warnings Maryon was finally called to count on the accusation that he was passing inferior work for sale. It was decided to terminate his agreement forthwith. His immediate reaction caused them to reconsider the legality of their move and consequently they withdrew and agreed that 'the

A medieval cross designed by H. J. Maryon.

minutes of the last meeting be annulled'. Maryon's response was to take an aggressive stance with the management committee, claiming in particular that; 'My position was made very difficult by the frequent visits of Mrs Rawnsley'. The Committee remained steadfast in their wish to terminate his appointment and Maryon eventually, despite continued claims for amendments, agreed to accept three months notice.[71] It is impossible to make a retrospective judgement on the merits of either side of this argument. The fact that Mrs Rawnsley was singled out for her implied interference is perhaps not surprising considering her own commitment and early responsibility in matters of quality control. Rawnsley had described how 'You will find the lady who started it all faithfully at her post no matter what the weather is, noting and criticising each piece of work, and deciding if it shall be passed and have the school stamp – a lozenge with the initials K.S.I.A. upon it'.[72] Delegating and entrusting this work to others was obviously undertaken with some reluctance especially when it was felt that high standards were not being applied.

In turn Robert Hilton was appointed in November 1904 for the salary of £200 with the agreement that he could bring his own foreman who would be paid 50*s*. a week. Although he was scheduled not to take up his appointment until the following July, by the May Hilton had already requested the resignation of some members in order to reduce the numbers and maintain standards. He also complained about the sanitation at the School. On both issues he was given the support of the Committee. The increasing commercial nature of the venture was reflected in the opening of a shop in Keswick as well in Chester where Hilton had been based. The perennial question of the designer's commitment to his own work in relationship to priority given to demands made by the School continued to occupy the minds of the Committee when this particular ledger, which recorded the 'Minutes' for the first ten years of the School, ended in June 1905. Robert Hilton was, however, to remain as Director for some seventeen years before he in turn was succeeded by G. A. Weeks.[73]

It is possible to perceive, in the early twentieth century, the way in which the School was able to evolve beyond its original Arts and Craft Movement base to allow it to continue and remain viable within the changing market place. In many ways this was made easier when Rawnsley became Canon of Carlisle in 1909 and moved away from Crosthwaite. More telling for the School, however, was the absence of his wife, whose contribution had been central to its formation in the early days. At the end of 1916 when a return to Crosthwaite was contemplated, Edith Rawnsley died. Rawnsley in acknowledging the tributes made to her described her as the 'foundress of the K.S.I.A.' and that she had 'put all her gifts at the service of the parish, and by her constant endeavour and help in the background, set me free to do what otherwise I could not have done for this neighbourhood and the public at large'.[74] Rawnsley died four years later and was buried in Crosthwaite churchyard where his epitaph reads: 'A helper of his time, Canon of Carlisle, Chaplain to the King, and thirty four years Vicar of the parish'.[75]

Conclusion

This account of the Keswick School of Industrial Arts has been written within the context of the Arts and Crafts Movement where the ideals of John Ruskin inspired those who were troubled by the consequences of industrialisation. From these ideals came the motivation for people like Albert Fleming, Marion Twelves, Hardwicke and Edith Rawnsley, and Annie Garnett to help people in rural areas to find work without having to move to the cities. They saw the resurrection of traditional craft industries as a way to counter impersonality and anonymity, traits seen as implicit within mass-produced goods. Sometimes, as seemed the case with Hardwicke Rawnsley, the idea and romance of a past era was re-invoked and applied to descriptions of their own enterprises. When Rawnsley described Ruskin's influence on the Home Art Industries in the Lake District he included this summary of the School rooms at Keswick.

> You will see the Art Director planning with sure hand how this or that metal problem is to be met. You will pass into the next room and mingle with the wood-carvers round their teacher, or on another evening you will watch the men with pencil in hand doing what they may to reproduce a branch of wild rose upon their drawing boards, or modelling a cast of a leaf in clay beneath the direction of their drawing teacher. You will open a door and find yourself in another room odorous with pitch and hissing loud as the red-hot bowl is tempered for its twentieth time. This is the abode of Vulcan and Aeolus *pro tem* ... Iron work has in this last year of the century been

An undated exhibition display of Keswick copper repoussé work and silverware.

added to the copper and brass work. Passing through this room you will enter the workshop where the silver work goes forward and beyond may chance to find an enameller's gas-stove red hot and a worker in enamel busy.[76]

Rawnsley's other concern, as present in his mission work in Soho and Bristol, had been to counter the evils of unemployment and drink. Although it is not possible to identify all who worked for the School, Rawnsley saw it as a success for the men of Keswick because 'they now have always something to turn to on a dull evening'. He also claimed on their behalf that 'We know nothing of the ideal before the mind of the promoters, this we know, that it is the grandest temperance agent in the place'.[77] His position as Vicar of the parish, County Councillor and member of numerous committees had given him a religious and public platform, which he used to both social and personal effect. The work at K.S.I.A., however, owed much more to the diligence and initial artistic enthusiasm of his wife Edith. It was she, the practitioner and organiser, who worked with a conscientious committee to provide the foundation for a School and industry, which was to continue until 1984. The tensions, referred to at the top of this piece, meant that the many young talented teachers and designers who came to the School, imbued it for only a short while with their talent and enthusiasm, before moving on to other challenges. Some in mistaking the ideals of the School, as somewhat amateur, used and exploited it; they too had to move on. For these reasons the continuity of the School may have been tested but while the core of craft workers from its home town remained steadfast, the visiting talents were a positive and welcome input inspiring products that were displayed in Liberty's and other shops and exhibitions throughout the land. It was an experiment that evolved to survive social and cultural changes unimaginable to its original founders, and deserves the attention of further research beyond the focus and remit of this chapter.

Acknowledgement

All photographs, with one exception, in this Chapter are kindly supplied by Cumbria Record Office, Carlisle from the Keswick Industrial Arts Collection. Copyright Untraceable.

Notes

1. Esther Wood, 'The Home Arts and Industries Exhibition at the Albert Hall' in *The Studio*, vol. 20 (1900), p. 78.
2. 'CW', 'Studio Talk', ibid.
3. Fiona MacCarthy, *The Simple Life C. R. Ashbee in the Cotswolds* (Lund Humphries, 1981), p. 30.
4. Ibid., n.23, p. 31.
5. John K. Walton, 'Canon Rawnsley and the English Lake District' in K. Hanley (ed.), *Armitt Library Journal* (Armitt Trust 1/1998), p. 1.
6. The archive of the Keswick School of Industrial Arts (K.S.I.A.), is housed in the Carlisle Record Office, ref DB/111/. My thanks to David Bowcock and the staff there in assisting my research.
7. Cited in E. T. Cook, *The Life of John Ruskin* (George Allen & Co., 1911), p. 187.
8. Ibid., p. 189.
9. Ibid.
10. Cited in H. D. Rawnsley, *Ruskin and The English Lakes* (James Maclehose & Sons, 1902), pp. 116–117.
11. Both his second wife's account in E. F. Rawnsley, *Canon Rawnsley* (James Maclehose & Sons, 1923) and M. Atkinson, 'Hardwicke Drummond Rawnsley, 1851–1920', M. Phil. thesis, University of Lancaster, 1993 have more details on these periods of his life.
12. Margaret Lane, *The Tale of Beatrix Potter* (Penguin, 1986), p. 45.
13. H. D. Rawnsley, *Ruskin and The English Lakes*, p. 116.
14. Ibid., p. 118.
15. Anthea Callen, *Angel in the Studio* (Astragal Books, 1979), p. 166. See

Chapter 6 for a fuller discussion on the role of women regarding 'Woodcarving, Furniture and Interior Design'.

16. See contemporary discussions in *The Art Journal* in 1861, 1872, 1896 and 1897.
17. Rawnsley, *Ruskin and The English Lakes*, p. 119. Edith Rawnsley's obituary notice also suggests 'she had studied in Verona, Florence and Venice'. *Westmorland Gazette*, January 6th, 1917. My thanks to Jean Turnbull for this reference.
18. Ibid.
19. Ibid., p. 121.
20. Ibid.
21. K.S.I.A. archive Carlisle Record Office DB/111/18.
22. Ibid.
23. J. Ruskin 'The Nature of Gothic' in Clive Wilmer (ed.), *Unto this Last* (Penguin, 1985), p. 84.
24. E. F. Rawnsley, *Canon Rawnsley* (Maclehose & Co, 1923), p. 67.
25. Ibid.
26. J. K. Walton, 'Canon Rawnsley and the English Lake District', p. 7.
27. K.S.I.A. archive DB/111/1.
28. K.S.I.A. archive. Cutting in album DB/111/93.
29. Ibid., *Carlisle Journal*, 22 May 1891.
30. Rawnsley, *Ruskin and The English Lakes*, p. 123.
31. Ibid., p. 122.
32. J. K. Walton, 'Canon Rawnsley and the English Lake District', p. 7.
33. See also Jennie Brunton, 'The late nineteenth-century revival of the Langdale linen industry', in Elizabeth Roberts (ed.), *A History of Linen in the North West* (CNWRS, Lancaster, 1998).
34. H. Rawnsley, *Ruskin and The English Lakes*, p. 143.
35. Article from *Handicrafts Magazine*, 1902 cited in F. A. Benjamin, *The Ruskin Linen Industry of Keswick* (Michael Moon, 1974), p. 28.
36. Ibid., p. 27.
37. Ibid., p. 28.
38. Ibid., p. 29.
39. K.S.I.A. archive. DB/111/93.
40. F. A. Benjamin, *The Ruskin Linen Industry of Keswick*, p. 11.
41. K.S.I.A. archive DB/111/1.
42. F. A. Benjamin, *The Ruskin Linen Industry of Keswick*, p. 11.
43. See Elizabeth Prickett, *Ruskin Lace and Linen Work* (B. T. Batsford Ltd, 1985).
44. Details from the Ruskin Collection, Reading University. Cited in F. A. Benjamin, *The Ruskin Linen Industry*, pp. 12–13.
45. Ibid.
46. Ibid., Citing the Crosthwaite Parish Magazine.
47. Ibid.
48. K.S.I.A. archive DB/111/1. This entry is significant for the first use of the typewriter in recording the 'Minutes': unfortunately it was not maintained.

49. Ibid.
50. For further details on the Guild see contemporary study by member Edith Hope Scott, *Ruskin's Guild of St George* (Metheun & Co., 1931), and a somewhat contentious discussion by Paul L. Sawyer, 'Ruskin and St George: the Dragon-Killing myth in "Fors Clavigera".' in *Victorian Studies*, vol. 23 (1979–80), pp. 5–28.
51. F. A. Benjamin, *The Ruskin Linen Industry of Keswick*, p. 20.
52. H. Rawnsley, *Ruskin and The English Lakes*, p. 144.
53. Cited in F. A. Benjamin, *The Ruskin Linen Industry of Keswick*, p. 19.
54. Ibid., p. 17.
55. K.S.I.A. archive DB/111/93. Newspaper cutting.
56. Cited in Sydney Chapman, 'Arts, Crafts and Heritage in Victorian Lakeland' in K. Hanley (ed.), *Armitt Library Journal* (Armitt Trust, 1/1998), p. 56.
57. Ibid.
58. K.S.I.A. archive DB/111/1.
59. Ibid., 2 November 1897 and 3 February 1898.
60. Ibid., 17 November 1896.
61. See *Westmorland Gazette*, 16 December 1893 and 15 October. 1898 where these achievements are recorded. My thanks to Eleanor Davidson for this reference.
62. K.S.I.A. archive DB/111/24.
63. T. Harrod, *The Crafts in Britain in the Twentieth Century* (Yale University Press, 1999), p. 7. (See also ref. below).
64. Ibid., DB/111/1, 23 March 1900.
65. Harold Stabler (1872–1945) warrants further space and research. In 1910 he was elected to serve as a member of the Arts and Crafts Society Exhibition hanging and selection committee and in 1915 was a founder member of The Design and Industries Association. See Tanya Harrod, *The Crafts in Britain in the Twentieth Century* (Yale University Press, 1999), pp. 71–72 for more information on his career. His connection with the K.S.I.A. continued in the 1930s when, besides his involvement with some designs for 'Pyrex', he also designed a collection of tableware made from 'Staybrite' steel and instigated a collaboration between J & J Wiggin and his old School in its development. These details from the slim Stabler file in the National Art Library.
66. K.S.I.A. archive DB/111/1.
67. H. Rawnsley, *Ruskin and The English Lakes*, p. 126.
68. K.S.I.A. archive DB/111/1, 4 May 1900.
69. Callen, *Angel in the Studio*, p. 161.
70. *The Catalogue for the 1903 Arts and Crafts Exhibition Society* (Chiswick Press) from a collection in the National Art Library at the V&A Museum. The catalogue also includes details of three exhibits designed and enamelled by Harold Stabler under the auspices of R. Llewellyn Rathbone.
71. K.S.I.A. DB/111/1, 29 August 1904.
72. H. Rawnsley, *Ruskin and The English Lakes*, p. 126.

73. E. F. Rawnsley, *Canon Rawnsley*, p. 68.
74. Ibid., p. 245.
75. Ibid., p. 264.
76. H. Rawnsley, *Ruskin and The English Lakes*, pp. 126–7.
77. Ibid., p. 128.

CHAPTER FIVE

Annie Garnett and The Spinnery at Bowness (The Windermere Industries)

> ... the fabrics, of pure linen, silk, and silk and linen mixed, woven by Miss Garnett, are delightful in colour and texture. There is a certain flame-red from which it is hard to tear the eye, and those in search of either dress materials or hangings will find things of great beauty and fitness here, while the embroideries are as various in character as they are pure in design.[1]

This review of the textiles produced in Bowness appeared following a 1906 exhibition at the prestigious Montague Fordham Gallery in the West End of London, and gives an early indication of the quality and range of products made at The Spinnery in the latter part of the nineteenth and early years of the twentieth century. In this chapter, besides discussing how the industry at The Spinnery developed, I want to highlight the significance of the work of women, like Annie Garnett (1864–1942), which is sometimes lost because of pre-conceived notions about the nature of their involvement with The Arts and Crafts Movement. As a result recognition of their organisational skills, creative ability and sheer quality of work has been undervalued and historically marginalised. As shown at both Keswick and in the Langdales, women participated and were central to the success of these industries but with the possible exception of Marion Twelves and Elizabeth Pepper, who held managerial positions, none occupied such an autonomous role within an enterprise as Annie Garnett. As she recorded in her unpublished diary on 8 September 1900; 'The burden on my shoulders was largely that my work, the Industry for the villagers, had only me to depend on for capital which I made by designing'.

While it may be my intention to show how successful Garnett was in terms of both the quality of her designs and managing the high standard of textile production, the issue of her gender had, and still has, impact on the value judgements affecting the question of how her work is subsequently viewed. She is not alone; the role of women in the context of the Arts and Crafts Movement is often viewed as somewhat ambiguous. The implication that they may have

A poster advertising an exhibition of Annie Garnett's work, held at the Lyceum Club in London founded in 1904. Design for the poster was probably by her friend and fellow Club member Alice B. Woodward, a renowned book illustrator.

been participating in something 'socially and artistically radical' is often moderated by the view, as expressed by Anthea Callen, that 'it in fact reproduced, perpetuated and thus reinforced dominant Victorian patriarchal ideology', which in turn has become part of our inherited history.[2] While elements of this viewpoint certainly appear to have relevance to Garnett I would argue, like Lynne Walker, 'that the extent to which the Arts and Crafts Movement reinforced patriarchal ideology is less clear-cut and rigid than was previously thought and instead of further alienating women, … [it] provided opportunities for women's paid employment, which often took place outside the home, in the public sphere'. As she continues; 'In many cases women's Arts and Crafts design work led to financial and personal independence well beyond previous experience, enhancing women's position and status in society in a much more fundamental way than has been conceded'.[3] While Callen might have expressed doubts as to how enabling this was, she has, in *Angel in the Studio*, her comprehensive study of women's participation in the Movement, shown 'how attractive work in the Arts and Crafts could be to single women of the middle class, who were prevented by the code of gentility from supporting themselves by work outside the home'.[4] This statement has a particular relevance when considering the experience of Annie Garnett within the context of late nineteenth-century Bowness.

Unfortunately no key business documents relating to ledgers, minute or account books remain today. This account has therefore been informed by researching her personal and published writings, samples of her work, photographs, sketchbooks, a visitors' book,

An undated studio photograph of Annie Garnett.

contemporary press reports and some business correspondence found within the archive at Abbot Hall in Kendal. Particular mention should be made of the diary she kept, sporadically, during the years 1899–1909, which she herself edited in preparation for a short autobiography. This, unfortunately, never came to fruition but its existence does mean the voice of Annie Garnett can be heard within the retelling of the history of her work at The Spinnery.

Annie Garnett was the second child and eldest daughter of six children (Edward, Annie, James, Frank, Wilhemina and Frances) born to William and Frances (nee Townson) Garnett. They lived at Fairfield, a house built in the early 1860s by the firm of Pattinsons, in the grounds above The Crown Hotel in Bowness. Both sides of the family owned land and these Garnetts, like those of Bloomsbury fame, claimed a connection with the Jesuit priest, Henry Garnett, who was hanged for failing to inform the authorities after hearing the confession of Guy Fawkes.[5] Fairfield had been provided for Annie's parents by her grandfather Edward Garnett, an eldest son who diversified from his agricultural roots when he built The Crown Hotel at the beginning of the nineteenth century. A description of Bowness in 1844 revealed the progress of a tourist trade even before the arrival of the railway in Windermere in 1847. William Pearson noted; 'Instead of an inn and a small tavern, it can now boast of five or six, two of them as large as palaces, and dignified with the name of Hotels'.[6] The hotel was initially managed by Thomas Cloudsdale and when Edward Garnett died in 1868, four years after Annie's birth, it was inherited by her father, William. However, it continued under the management of the Cloudsdale family, whose surname frequently prefixed the Crown Hotel in nineteenth-century descriptions. Only for a brief period prior to William's death did the family appear to have any direct involvement with the hotel.

Annie Garnett's father appears to have spent his working life as a land agent, managing the large estate of Lord Bradford, north of Windermere. His three sons were educated at the public school at St Bees while the three sisters, of whom only one was to marry, were educated at home. William Garnett had an extensive library at Fairfield, which reflected his particular enthusiasm for illuminated manuscripts. This, together with his interest in architecture, may have encouraged his friendship with John Ruskin. As a friend he was to seek the opinion of this renowned art critic about his own daughter's artistic skills. Annie, herself recalled the occasion, when recording news of Ruskin's death in 1900.

> ... Father had been over at Brantwood; and Mr Ruskin after showing him his treasures criticised some of my paintings and was very pleased with a study of roses, not an arrangement, but single studies; and also with a little landscape I had sent to him to see. It was a great encouragement to me, and how I longed to go on with my paintings: but it was not to be, except in almost stolen moments as a precious recreation. This was when we were living at St Bees; all were at home and there was so much to do in the house.[7]

The family stayed on the coast at St Bees for a short time during a period of her father's ill-health when, as indicated by her diary entry, Annie's time was occupied mainly with domestic duties. Despite her father's apparent support and respect for her talents Annie was not to receive an Art School training, as some contemporary articles in *The Art Journal* were advocating. These articles sought to persuade readers, fathers in particular, to show their concern for the future welfare of women by preparing them for some form of suitable employment, should circumstances make it necessary for them to earn money. Such a concern was initiated by the census revelation that there were far more women in the population than men and those who found themselves 'surplus' and consequently unable to secure their 'true vocation' as wives and mothers should be prepared for such an eventuality. One solution, for women from the so called 'respectable classes', suggested by *The Art Journal* articles was to consider the suitability of art work.[8] It would seem,

A watercolour sketch by Annie Garnett dated 1906.

however, that Annie's father complied with the traditional dominant view that:

> For a woman to be earning money when it was not absolutely necessary was seen as a humiliating reflection on the man whose role it was to provide for her. It was manifestly inconceivable that a woman should see earning her own living as a simple matter of achieving self-respect and independence, something which for men was not merely taken for granted, but considered as part of their duty.[9]

Whatever his wishes, his comparatively early demise at the age of fifty-six in 1888 would have left his unmarried daughter of twenty four beholden to her brothers. For Garnett, a women who believed that 'The first thing to be done is I think for a girl to be taught to think ...' this would seem a somewhat untenable situation.[10]

Later in that same year she was to accompany Colonel Ridehalgh and his daughter, Alice, on the maiden voyage of the 'Ibis' from Dundee to Antwerp. The Colonel as one of the co-founders, and four-times Commodore, of the Royal Windermere Yacht Club owned several large yachts including the 'Britannia' which was used to entertain those who were obviously part of the elite social circle that revolved around Lake Windermere.[11] Garnett's brother Edward was to marry Alice Ridehalgh which might appear to confirm her own inclusion in this social circle. However, despite appearances I believe Garnett's position, because of her family, gender and marital status, to be more nebulous than this classing by association might suggest. Her own family background, through her mother and father, connected them to the old order of farmers and gentry but their newer association through the hotel was with the developing commercial tourist trade from which subsequent generations appeared to distance themselves. The success of this trade had, however, secured the family home, Fairfield, where Annie lived with her mother and younger sister Frances for the majority of her life. In 1909, when her mother died, the hotel was sold to Richard Rigg, probably the most renowned of all lakeland hoteliers; but provision had been made for the two sisters to remain at Fairfield. Despite her regional grounding, however, Garnett frequently chose to mix with the new 'off-comers' society, where women of educated and moneyed backgrounds were able to share cultural aspirations and she had the possibility of finding patrons. It would seem, however, that in doing this she occupied a somewhat tenuous position on the margins of both the old and new social circles found around the small provincial town of Bowness. This role was exacerbated by her status as a spinster and was reflected later in her unpublished diary by feelings of isolation. If this interpretation is seen as somewhat negative then conversely it should be remembered that this very marginality meant she was not so confined by conventions of class and behaviour. In this instance a strong sense of self, together with a need for some sort of independent outlet, was to help her in developing her own way of being.

While there is no clear picture of Annie Garnett's financial situation, there is evidence that this process began shortly after her father's death, when she visited an Arts and Crafts exhibition, while on her trip to Belgium. This led her to record her disappointment in her compatriots when she wrote; 'The English section ... the poorest, so plain'.[12] The second and seemingly most significant influence came through a visit made closer to home in the Langdales. As she recalled;

> It was at the end of the 80's that I went with Bun to see the little spinning home at Elterwater founded in 1883 by Mr Fleming on Ruskin's writings chiefly. I was literally set down in the old world never to be again free from it and I found myself longing to be surrounded by ancient Industry, were it spinning, or weaving, or carving, or any other art that went to make up the home-life of long ago ...[13]

Putting ideas into practice

The order book for the Langdale Linen Industry does indeed verify that she bought three yards of linen in July 1889 and later in that year purchased a Spinning Book.[14] Her first publication in 1896, *Notes on Handspinning*, was to reveal the depth of interest and knowledge she acquired about the history of her chosen craft but more immediate practical issues occupied her initial plans. Annie Garnett, herself, outlined how things were started with a class in Bowness in 1890, in a long reflective diary entry she made in 1899.

> ... I became acquainted with the Brownsons, Mr Brownson was the Curate and his wife was much interested in art work; she too had a great desire to teach our villagers spinning and together we started our industry. Mr Brownson as secretary of the Art School organized lessons in Spinning and Embroidery and engaged Mrs Pepper the manageress of the Langdale Spinning Home to teach – the class was much larger than we expected and I took the spinning pupils, that Mrs Pepper might give all her time to the Embroiderers.

To hold such a class was in keeping with Ruskin's basic ideology in promoting traditional crafts in rural areas. Annie Garnett herself attended woodcarving classes and had subsequently carved some of her own bedroom furniture. One might speculate that she had attended classes at Wray or Ambleside where Edith and Hardwicke Rawnsley had promoted a similar revival. The presence of Elizabeth Pepper endorses the connection between the development of work in Bowness and the existing industry in the Langdales. Garnett's confidence in conducting the spinning lessons, herself, reflects a competence borne out of her new abilities that needed to be carried forward. The next step was recorded in her diary as:

> In January 1891 we discussed ways and means. 'I was lifted into action' by a Postal Order from Ernest Goddard [a relation through marriage] who had been staying with us and heard our discussions. Having this money in hand we must begin. We ordered two wheels, Winnie and I guaranteeing payment. We had a grand anonymous gift; – a loom, 6 wheels, warping frame and expenses for six months. Mrs Brownson was to be secretary, I, treasurer – the management to be equally shared between us. Mr Fleming, founder of the Langdale Industry was 'pleased to lend his name as President, Mr Brownson was Vice-President'.

Albert Fleming's presence, within what was then named The Windermere Industries, not only echoes the Langdale association but provides further evidence, through his own friendship and support from Ruskin, to fuel speculation that John Ruskin, himself was the donor of the 'grand anonymous gift'. He was known to the family, Annie Garnett refers to conversations she had with him, and Ruskin had made similar practical contributions before, as he did with the mill at Laxey in the Isle of Man.

With the equipment in place Garnett continued to practise her craft. The Langdale order book recorded several more of her purchases of flax during 1891, when she also submitted her work for public scrutiny. Her reward from the Kendal Arts, Crafts and Loan Exhibition included a first prize for Handspun Flax Yarn presented by Albert Fleming, and a first and two second prizes for artistic needlework as well as a second prize for her embroidered curtain. Garnett was to write later that the women of Elterwater, '... bemoaning the fact that the prize had not fallen to their lot, were quite consoled in remembering the part they had taken in making the thread, "but we larned her" they were overheard to remark quite cheerfully'.[15] This particular year was noted in the diary as when 'definite work began in 1891 – April the eleventh to be exact' with the first commercial order which '... we received from an American, Mrs Pierpont-Morgan, for 2 dozen fine linen towels ...'.

Some difficulty was recorded in attracting women to work for the industry 'as people could not understand the idea of bringing back the old wheels'.[16] As at Langdale no charge was made in teaching pupils how to spin and once they were proficient they were allowed to take a spinning wheel home, again at no charge, and were paid as outworkers once the flax had been spun into linen thread. By 1896 Garnett recorded in *Notes on Handspinning*, '... we have now twenty-one wheels lent out to the cottagers, and many women now own their own wheels'.[17]

An example of Garnett's artistic embroidery.

In the absence of any documentation to clarify the specific aims of the industry, as are present, for example, with the Keswick School of Industrial Arts, it is difficult to understand why there should be the early differences, regarding its commercial and financial nature, which emerged within the management team. As is often the case these appeared to arise through poor communication, personality differences and misunderstandings. Garnett recorded in her diary:

> We had not worked long before a very unhappy time started – Mrs Brownson arranged for the gift of an Altar Cloth to the Church unknown to me – the weaving department was under my control, the embroidery under Mrs Brownsons. It was from the weavers I heard of this gift; I refused at the time to allow it for we were unable to pay our way and I could not see it was right that we should give, even to the Church. I, too was finding money to carry on the work and, it may be, indeed is most likely, I was hurt through not being consulted in the matter. From this time, till the Brownsons left, a year or so later, there was no peace – by every effort they tried to prevent it; even to threatening the starting of a separate industry which I knew must be the one to prosper. I have all the letters from, and copies of letters to this remarkable pair. We formed a large committee – 34 in number – to spread the interest. There was a great attempt on their side to propose only Church people – so long as they would be, or

> had been helpful to us I was for any; no matter what religious views they held; each side had to give way in several cases.[18]

Again there are no records to name this somewhat large committee but the situation was resolved when the Brownsons were allocated a new parish at Compton Greenfield, near Bristol. Garnett's resilience had paid off, justifiably so as she felt when learning that an industry they went on to start in Compton Greenfield failed to attract much support and lasted only a short time. Following their departure Miss Rawson, the vicar's daughter, was appointed as secretary but ill health and frequent absences from Bowness meant she was 'secretary only in name'. As for the large committee, they rarely met and few seemed interested or familiar with the running of the business and so the initial constitution (whatever that might have been) was dissolved as from 1 November 1898. Garnett recorded; 'When the industry dissolved we had had no meeting for 3 full years – I had borne the whole work and found all the capital. It could scarcely be said I was hampered or hindered by a committee. It was however a useless affair and better dismissed'.[19]

It was therefore through determination, resilience, self-belief and the evolution of a situation that Garnett found herself in charge of this industry, a somewhat unusual position for a woman at the end of the nineteenth century. She was not therefore without her critics and seemed particular troubled by the remarks of a family acquaintance, Dr MacDonald. While expressing approval for her work, which was deemed to help others, he accused her of being 'utterly selfish' by using her artistic abilities to earn money. As Garnett angrily confided to her diary; '... if I were not able to earn something, my usefulness would end for my "approved" work could not exist without capital'. It would seem that Dr MacDonald, like others, presumed that Garnett's involvement with this industry should be purely philanthropic, and that to earn money cast aspersions on both herself and her family's class and social position. Such remarks also provide evidence for believing that Garnett developed the duality of producing simple 'hand-spun' textiles alongside sophisticated silks not only to comply with her ideological and creative beliefs but also to mediate an acceptable social perception of herself and her work within Bowness society.

It is worth noting that when she published *Notes on Handspinning* she appended her name with the description 'Co-Founder of the Windermere Industry and Honorary Manageress of the Spinning and Weaving Department of the same'. In future publications she either omitted her name altogether or used a monogram of her initials in a somewhat art nouveau style. This move to anonymity was justified in an interview, when the journalist reported:

> Miss Garnett has an objection to have her name mentioned in connection with this venture. It is the work and the purpose that should tell, that should be praised and honoured and not persons.[20]

Finding herself alone at the head of this industry she nevertheless remained undaunted in her efforts and recorded these words which reflect an acceptance of responsibility with determination and caution.

> I carry the work on just the same but have more helpers and am developing and enlarging it as far as capital permits. It is scarcely possible to say to what extent it might be developed but I am anxious not to loose[sic] touch with any part of it and if it increases much more rapidly I am afraid this may occur – capital, or want of it seems the only brake.[21]

In her differences with the Brownsons, Annie Garnett had one very important factor in her favour. The spinning and weaving equipment central to the enterprise had been set up in some outbuildings within the grounds of her family home at Fairfield. The Crown Hotel had been used for some of the earliest lessons providing more space and formality than a family home but it was indeed fortunate that a separate space was available for a more

Centre of the Windermere Industries; The Spinnery in the grounds of Fairfield, Bowness.

One of publicity photographs taken by Brunskill & Co. This one includes spinning wheels, examples of work and Annie Garnett's beloved dog, Mike.

permanent venue for the business. In an article published in the *Art Workers' Quarterly* in 1905, she described the premises known as The Spinnery, which had once been used by her father as an office and workshop, and were later to require further expansion.

> The Spinnery is a roomy building standing at the entrance to Fairfield. It was originally an office and loft, with stable and coach-house below; the latter made useful weaving sheds, whilst the room and loft above made excellent workrooms. Soon, however, they were growing less; there was scarcely room to move amongst the stores of flax and wool and silk; spun yarn, stuffs, embroideries; looms and wheels; so a great weaving shed and extra rooms were added, rooms having the long low windows beloved of weavers ... In the warping-room may be seen at times a mill bearing a silken burden of 11,000 odd ends, each 56½ yards long ...

Many photographs were taken of the workshops, weaving-room and studio areas by the local photographer Brunskill and used to publicise the notion of integrating the designs and textiles produced at The Spinnery by the Windermere Industries into a domestic setting. The environment in which these goods were produced was used, as with other enterprises affiliated to the Arts and Crafts Movement, to emphasise the difference between this mode of producing individual hand-crafted textiles and the mass produced ones from the mills of Lancashire and Yorkshire as well as further afield.

Garnett's association with the movement's ideology and the thinking of Ruskin and Morris, which acknowledged the importance of individual artistic craft work, was made obvious in one of her earlier publications in 1904 when she wrote:

> I cannot enter into the vast issues that surround us through the false steps taken when Art was parted from Craftsmanship; ... art is not

> to be looked on as a separable thing divided up into the painting of pictures, the writing of music, the weaving of brocades, or embroidering of garments; carving of panel, tooling of metal, or writing of books; the same laws and the same truths are for each, it is only the manner of expression that is different.
>
> To have the most perfect craftsmanship it is necessary to cultivate every faculty; to know art in the whole-minded way; to search out truth in all things; and to keep the mind fixed high.[22]

At the same time she abhorred the effects of industrialisation and the increasing urbanisation of the population, which also identified her with the 'Back to the Land' movement. Although she may have written of the need to have 'good honest ideas on all social questions; broad lines with plenty of margin for the individual conscience',[23] she was not in accord with Morris and his move towards revolutionary change. Instead she concurred with Ruskin's call for a return to the old sense of social order, writing rather idealistically of 'a peasant class' which 'has vanished, has gone to the making of densely packed towns' deeming them to have 'tired of the old peaceful life, with its sufficiency of work and enough to live on ...'.[24] On the many occasions when she did leave Bowness to travel abroad and to visit major towns and cities in this country, it was always viewed as something of an ordeal expressed most succinctly following a visit to Liverpool and Bolton.

> Towns I hate; loathe them; I am never happy amongst smoke, and fog ... and crowds: at any moment I could take to my heels and fly to green fields and hedgerows; anywhere where the houses are not huddled together in hideous mass: where the smells will not stifle one; where the folks are clean, where I may feel myself. I think if I lived long in [a] town my whole being must change; it has an ill effect on me; and it makes one wonder sometimes if my life and my ways are not too simple ...[25]

She was indeed fortunate to live in such a beautiful part of the country and to have the security of living in the same house for her whole life. She did, nevertheless appreciate the need for change, writing '... it is absolutely necessary to have change; not for one's health sake only [but] it prevents one getting in grooves, growing narrower ...'.[26] Despite admitting to some of the temptations of an increasingly commercial world, in essence she remained unequivocal declaring; 'A country life is the life to live; in touch with God, nature controlling; surrounded with Nature; in the very midst of Nature; part of Nature'.[27] It is this theme that interweaves the pages of her diary reflecting its intrinsic importance to Garnett. Nature was the

As indicated by Garnett's writing this is a Work-room at The Spinnery.

main source of inspiration for her poems and prose writing and, as outlined in the next section, it was the colours and forms she observed in the countryside around her that inspired her textile creations.

Creating and Producing Textiles at The Spinnery

When Garnett completed the Census of Production Papers for the Board of Trade in 1924 she stated that in her business she was 'Working from an Artists [sic] point of view ...'. This statement from someone who as her sister Frances verified in 1952 '... had no oral [formal] training – either in design, weaving or colouring'[28] says much about the opportunities afforded by the Arts and Crafts Movement for those not privileged to access the hierarchical world of fine art. As already stated she did not attend Art School; however, the many sketches and small watercolours to be found in the archive demonstrate her ability to convey the ambience of a landscape through her choice of muted colours which were then applied to the textiles made at The Spinnery. Another successful element was her eye for form, made most apparent through pencil sketches. Close attention to the shape of a plant and flower, before they were made part of an embroidery or textile design, indicated her wish to replicate a somewhat more natural form than that found in the stylised work of the Glasgow School of Art. It is also apparent that Garnett shared her father's interest in architecture with a number of sketches of churches and other buildings with special attention made to individual design features. Other sources for designs were found through the expanding world of print and the effect of magazines like *The Studio* and *The English Illustrated Magazine* should not be underestimated, as they certainly inspired readers like Garnett. A competition relating to monograms in one issue of *The Studio* seemed to have generated several pages in one of her sketch books.

Besides her artistic talents, Garnett was keen to have a thorough knowledge of the whole process of textile production. For this reason she was critical of Joseph King's work at the, now more renowned, Haslemere and the Peasants' Arts Industry. Following his visit to The Spinnery in 1899 she recorded:

> They only use machine made yarns and keep 6 girls weaving. The whole affair seems too limited. He has spent over £200 in building a weaving shed he says. I am afraid he has started at the wrong end – the weaving before the spinning: and the building before the work. It is better, I think, to begin at the beginning and climb up.[29]

In the same year Mrs Caine from the Utah Silk Commission visited providing further evidence of the networks that connected these industries, nationally and internationally. Garnett recorded that she felt encouraged to grow her own mulberry bushes and so produce her own silk worms 'and from these I intend trying to spin silk direct instead of buying it carded by machinery and in the silver state'.[30] Garnett's silk spinning skills had been initiated, it appears, in the production of her sister Wilhemina's wedding dress when she noted, 'it took me 17 hours to fill the first bobbin and five and a half to fill the last and I spun in all twenty bobbins'. More significantly; 'It was the beginning of our silk industry'.[31] Several references are made to Garnett's own early weaving, carried on alongside that in the workshop. This included; 'We have almost finished setting up a loom in my bed-room and in a few [days] I hope to start weaving a silk web. By the time that is done I hope to have enough yarn of my own spinning ready to weave'.[32] It was, however, following Mrs Caine's visit that first mention was made of the presence of 'the experienced weaver'. Garnett had been inspired to implement methods for saving thread in the warp and encouraged 'Mr White' to experiment. She recorded the outcome in her diary:

> White said 'It's an impossibility, no man living can do it; if any man could, I'm the man that could'; and he was. I stood by him, insisting on every additional inch being woven, helping with the heddles, as

The Weaving Sheds at The Spinnery, including two of the male employees.

> he made them the more contrary to get the knots through, feeling I know that the thing was going to be done; but determined to prove to me it could not. Inch by inch was woven and a great mass of hand-spun yarn saved, all he said was 'Well I knew if it could be done I was the man to do it', and so in future each web will, I hope convince him of the uselessness of beginning a task with the settled conviction that it is an impossibility to accomplish it. I have had many discussions with him on the subject of this waste; but was never able to show him before how it could be avoided.

During the period 1891 to 1914 when the bulk of silk, linen and tweed textiles were produced; it was the throwan, 'perhaps the most interesting of all stuffs woven at The Spinnery' that earned her reputation and gained the most attention.[33] In this she set out to achieve 'natural effects in the material' and recorded 'I designed my first throwan from the white bark of a birch against a blue sky' and 'the "thistle-bloom" throwan from the common hedge-row thistle with the pollen standing on it as it is in the autumn . . .'.[34] A throwan was made from a linen warp and a silk weft. By varying the weight of either the warp or the weft a coarse or fine finish was achieved.[35] A range of sample pieces in the archive which were attached to strips of brown paper indicate the range of colours available. On the green spectrum there are sixteen variations ranging from 'peacock', which was a green silk on a turquoise linen warp, to 'kingfisher', to 'fir trees in shadow', to 'hedge sparrow egg'. Of the blue spectrum, there are twenty three colour-way samples, again named after their source of inspiration; ranging from 'wild hyacinth' to 'larkspur' which was a bright purple silk on blue linen, to 'distant heather', a deep pink silk on blue linen. In colours working from orange to brown, there are twenty four samples with names like 'heart of furnace', 'flame', 'brown kingfisher', 'Bronze', 'oyster shell' and 'maize'. In red, seventeen samples range from 'autumn tints', 'dark pink lupin' to 'rose pink'. In this way Garnett was able to develop a wide range of throwans; not only by combining two colours to increase the colour-ways but also by varying the weight of thread as well as introducing a patterned herringbone design. Throwans varied in price from sixteen shillings to twenty seven shillings and sixpence a yard.

Although it was stated that she received no formal art school training, in November 1900 she attended a course at Yorkshire College in Leeds. Here, under the guidance of Professor Beaumont, she recorded that she 'learned lots I wanted to know; worked out a small design on point paper; cut some of the cards for it; and wove a piece of material – quite a fine brocade …'. Armed with this knowledge she recorded her intention to buy a Jacquard loom for £30, a purchase which is verified by photographs of the workshop. Practical demonstrations also formed an important part of many exhibitions where technical knowledge, gleamed through correspondence courses, could be viewed and clarified. This, as Garnett was to note of one Home Arts Exhibition experience, was not always given with good grace, contrary to how she perceived the ethos of the association which was 'to bring workers together that they might instruct and help others as one would have thought they should enjoy doing in the brotherhood …'.[36]

Garnett's commitment to the enterprise, as her diary revealed, was tested severely during this year. Despite all her actions she complained of 'a weary summer and now autumn is with us: our affairs have gone from bad to worse in one way; now surely the wheel will turn and things will be brighter …' and observed 'it is all very well for folks to say money is not everything: my experience is that money is a great deal and that the want of it can impose hardships well-nigh unbearable'. This diary entry, left uncut by her editorial scissors, provides an almost unique opportunity to glimpse the financial realities for Garnett during this period of the business. As mentioned earlier she earned money for the industry through her designing but such a necessity meant, as she related in the same entry that, 'you cannot give *only* of your best …'. There is little doubt that Annie Garnett was responsible for all the design work at The Spinnery as applied in both the production of the sophisticated handloom textiles as well as the embroidered linen for domestic use. A review of her work for the Home Arts and Industries Exhibition in 1905 conceded that while the Windermere weavings were better known than the embroideries, 'the needlework, however, is quite as distinguished as the weaving for their exquisite colour and beauty of design'.[37]

The needlework produced included the self-patterned white work, achieved by the pulling and drawing of threads as well as needle weaving which created a lacey effect within the linen cloth. Many of these skills were practised by the Langdale Linen Industry where Garnett probably received her first lessons. As with other crafts she developed this art producing detailed instructions, for what she called Norwegian work, to reflect her exacting standards which she intended to copyright. Within the Lake District such work was known as both Greek Lace and the more renowned Ruskin Lace which had a dark red or blue silk backing.[38]

Her embroidery designs which were largely influenced by 'some of the Southern European embroideries, which are so popular now' were used by Liberty's.[39] In response to the increasing demand for 'Home Needlework', Liberty's produced a number of pamphlets which contained paper patterns to transfer onto fabric. Although many of these were not attributed to particular designers, Garnett recorded 'I had a letter from their manager saying how much he admired some of the work he had just bought and wishing I would send him a selection up oftener'.[40] Like Liberty's, The Spinnery also supplied embroidery silks for exclusive use with their own designs. A range of colours were attached to cards bearing her logo with the following specification:

> The embroidery threads are made specially for the Spinnery work, and are dyed to take up the colour effects in nature that are part of the design. At the request of many clients who have enjoyed using

A piece of embroidery displaying Garnett's ability to use her knowledge of plant form, here Grape Hyacinth, to make stylised designs.

> them in work, prepared at the Spinnery, they may be bought apart from the designed work, but only by clients, as it is not our wish to sell embroidery silks in the ordinary way.

Garnett's designs, however, did not always meet with universal acclaim as recorded following an Home Arts and Industries Exhibition at the Albert Hall in May 1901: 'The embroidery and design judges [comment] that we have advanced in design and work. As a rule they do not like my design which Mr H. Rathbone next stallholder to me, thinks is a very healthy sign: they are certainly very unlike Home Art Design and he prefers individuality . . .'.[41] In Bowness the embroidery work was given to outworkers, 'chiefly village girls; tradesmen's daughters, who work in their spare time; or College women and girls; I have tried poor ladies, a class that needs help more than any other, but they are most disappointing; hemmed in by tradition, and so hopeless'.[42] Further evidence of Garnett's quest to produce something other than the ordinary was borne out by an undated article, fixed in a scrapbook, entitled 'The Work of the Women's World'. It reads

> The woven stuff is given out to the tradesmen's daughters, who take it to their homes to embroider, and incidentally their taste undergoes the most extraordinary transformation in the training enforced by the execution of the beautiful designs Miss Garnett creates.

In 1903 Garnett showed examples from both sides of the business, for the first time, at the Arts and Crafts Exhibition Society. These included the hand-woven silks and throwans together with a large embroidered screen, mounted in ebony and priced at £31 10*s*. 0*d*. She produced four such screens but this one was based on the ubiquitous peacock feather. It had three panels, the central one having seven 'eye' feathers and the outer panels, five. In all, over a dozen pieces were selected for the 1903 exhibition and were displayed with the names of individual spinners and weavers, names which included George Paterson and T. Erskine.

As mentioned at the beginning of this chapter, her work was also sold through the Fordham Gallery and it was through this outlet that the acclaimed actress Eleanor Duse purchased an 'early Victorian throwan' which was used in a 1903 production of *La Dame aux Camellias* together with, as Garnett recorded, 'a great coverlet of our white silk with a border of the golden pheasant or furnace throwan'. Also on stage in either a production of *As You Like It* or *Twelfth Night* was Ellen Terry wearing a dress made out of 'distant heather throwan'.[43]

Further evidence of the growing expertise within The Spinnery workforce can be gauged by the presence of Max Schaffhausen. In the 1903 Arts and Crafts Exhibition a piece of brocaded damask silk, 'executed' by him had been designed by Luther Hooper, a key figure in the revival of twentieth century hand-loom weaving, who was at the time, based at Haslemere.[44] A year later it is, however, his other talents which affect Schaffhausen's terms of employment at The Spinnery and warrant a reference in Garnett's diary. In February 1904 she wrote:

> It is all very well having a musical weaver but as he very often played all night he never did, or very rarely, a proper amount of weaving in

The Peacock Screen exhibited at the Arts and Crafts Exhibition Society in 1903.

> the day; so he is going to give up weaving for music which is much the best thing to do if he loves it best; and I will employ him as I need, to weave at so much per yard.

Her love of music and her own playing of the cello in a local orchestra may have made her more sympathetic than other employers. The 1910 edition of *Kelly's Directory*, however, still records his profession as a weaver.

Arthur Astle also joined the workforce at The Spinnery in around 1904. He was to be Garnett's longest serving weaver and was known to have come from Macclesfield, renowned for its own silk industry. In 1906 he was attributed with executing a 'white samite' designed by Garnett which was shown at the Arts and Crafts Exhibition Society at the Grafton Galleries and priced at £2. The samite was based on a medieval fabric using gold, silver or aluminium threads woven into a silk warp. From one of the many stock and sample cards sent out from The Windermere Industry at The Spinnery, a small sample of an aluminium samite, reveals that it was twenty four inches wide and cost forty two shillings a yard. This made it one of the most expensive in her range of textiles. Katherine Grasset, of the London School of Weaving, produced a similar fabric which she described as 'silk and aluminium tissue'.[45]

Experimentation in producing these textiles was the result of research and there is evidence that, like William Morris, Garnett studied the structure of earlier textiles. Sketchbooks in the archive document a 1905 visit to both the British and South Kensington Museums when she recorded the detailed structure of an early fourteenth century pattern woven with a thick gold thread into linen as well as an Italian seventeenth century ground satin pattern in a heavy weave. Further research into and the naming of the 'samite' is revealed through her correspondence with Davina Waterson who wrote; 'I enclose the allusion to *Samite* in Mallory's Morte d'Arthur, and in looking through the catalogue of [the] Dulwich Picture Gallery I came across [the] enclosed …'. A later letter reported 'nothing has come of the Assyrian research … [but] I enclose the result of the samite search as far as it has gone. Are we on the right tack?' Again writing from an address near the British Museum she added; 'Here is a little bit more re *Samite*, but with regard to the ancient representations of spinning I have not been so successful …'. Confirmation that this information was provided on a professional basis comes with the request for payment: 'All that I have found comes to 7/6 w[hic]h is not, I know, to you exorbitant as you understand how much time the mere searching takes up'.[46]

On an earlier occasion in May 1901, Garnett recorded another

The desk where many of the designs came to fruition at The Spinnery.

visit to South Kensington when she enlisted the help of an attendant in her research into 'Coptic and some Italian weaving'. Having secured a future appointment 'to see a little loom uncovered and also some different weavings' she declared 'It is grand to think matters are so arranged that it is possible to learn all one wants to learn. Here in this great country's museum with its store of ancient art and knowledge; and authorities ready to give you of their knowledge ...'.[47] To accompany her on her return visit she invited Godfrey Blount and his wife, of the Peasant Art Society based in Haslemere. This despite her derogatory opinion of him as ' a man I dislike ... [and who] declares it never occurred to him in any of his numerous visits to study textiles at the museum to ask if there was any one who could help him ...'. She went on to congratulate the magnanimity of her gesture as 'knowledge belongs to no one individual I thought; it is God's gift for all; and no one has any right to withhold it'. Her contact with the Museum led to a request for her to send them some of her own fabrics. In responding she recorded;

> I wonder what they will think of them: they cannot be compared with the old world things. Only I cannot help saying the colourings are lovely – colour I revel in – and can get dyes full of light and bleed different shades and different spun yarns together there is a delight and interest without end in the things.[48]

Garnett's attention to detail in reproducing and using a combination of colours found in nature, through the services of dyers both local and those of more national repute like Thomas Wardle, was fundamental to the particular reputation she gained for the work at The Spinnery.

Her research into fine muslin, which had been somewhat frustrated by an inability to get near enough to a Mummy in the British

Museum, in order 'to discover the weave of the linen they were wrapped in' was to be fulfilled in an unusual fashion. Following a visit to the bleach works and spinning mills at Newton-le-Willows and the weavers at Lowton in the Leigh area of Lancashire, Garnett was invited to tea by the owner's wife. She recorded

> After tea ... Mrs Clegg showed us a mummy's head, her husband had found it in one of the Rock caves in Egypt: it is gruesome to a degree but fascinating; the hair, that curious reddish tinge all ancient hair seems to have ... now I held a piece of mummy cloth in my hand: a real piece, some 4,000 years old; the warp is much finer than the weft, giving it a curious rippled look, like tiny sea waves, one trying to get to the other. I have made a piece of 'Mummy Cloth' at the Spin: and it looks very like the original.[49]

From the finest of weaves with the somewhat ethereal name of 'woven air' to the heavier tweeds, Annie Garnett's fabrics reflected her technical knowledge and her attention to design and colour which was informed by her close observation of both the surrounding landscape and the wide spectrum of plants growing in her garden. An extract from an article published in *The Pall Mall Gazette* in February 1911 provides a comprehensive view of the textiles sold during The Spinnery's peak years.

> The weaving of samites has greatly developed, and there are now produced rich stuffs of gold, silver, and aluminium that make ideal fabrics for court trains, and for draperies and other uses on great occasions ...
>
> The woven-air scarves are still made in the same quantities; and to pass to sterner things, never have there been so many orders for hand-spun woollens as during the last few months; the colour schemes obtained from the scotch moors, a couple of years ago have gradually developed into interesting homespuns, and many a sportsman shoulders his gun on what was originally drawn from the moors he tramps on ...
>
> Silk handkerchiefs, too, are made – dainty things that look too ethereal to use, but are said to be useful; great square silk mufflers; ties of all sorts, for both men and women; silks for dust cloaks; satins for bridal gowns; brocades for stately gowns; and every kind of silk for day and evening gowns ...

This description also gives some indication of the nature of her customers and in the absence of an order book her leather-bound visitors' book, which bears Garnett's initials and the motto 'Diligentia et Honore', provides further evidence. Two hundred and forty two names appear in the initial period from April 1899 to the beginning of 1900. In some years these entries were intensified, reflecting the exhibitions Garnett held at Bowness prior to taking her textiles to the London or Leeds venues for the national shows. On 14 April 1900, for example, there were fifty two signatures including Arthur W. Simpson. From further afield, visitors were listed from America, Canada, South Africa, Europe, South America and Australia; as reflected in the advertising for the Crown Hotel, Garnett's business might also have claimed to have been 'Patronized by Royalty, by American Presidents and by the Aristocracy'.[50] It is perhaps not surprising to see also the names of northern industrialists who commissioned the building of second and holiday homes in the Lake District. These included Elizabeth and Edward Holt, later Lord Mayor of Manchester, for whom Baillie Scott had built Blackwell as well as the Lord Mayor of Leeds, Currer Briggs. Garnett's friendship with Mrs Currer Briggs, based also on their shared love of music, was recorded in her diary and personal correspondence as was her visit and admiration for the incomplete Broad Leys, the house designed for them by C. F. A. Voysey. This friendship extended to visits to Leeds for the musical festivals and exhibitions where Garnett was a house guest alongside the renowned architect. This social milieu provided an entrée into some of wealthier homes in the land which in turn became market places for Garnett's textiles. An informal letter from Henry Bentinck at Underley Hall, for example, thanked her for silks she had sent which he intended to take with him to Scotland to show his friends. This also confirms that he, Lord Bective, like other family members took an active interest in the textile industries at Langdale and Bowness. In fact Garnett attributed Lady Bective with providing her with her first 'Danish Loom' and showing her how to weave.[51]

The most prestigious and significant signature to be found within the visitors' book was unquestionably Queen Victoria's daughter, the Princess Schleswig-Holstein, whom Garnett had already been introduced to at the national exhibitions. As the President of the Royal School of Art Needlework, founded in 1872, the Princess was influential in promoting this work as 'suitable employment for gentlewomen, and restoring ornamental needlework to the high place, it once held among the decorative arts'.[52] Unfortunately there is no corresponding diary entry, with her visit on 25 September 1908, to reflect Garnett's feelings on this royal visit to The Spinnery.

Further royal patronage, however, in the person of Queen Alexandra, was responsible for the commissioning of one of the most lavish pieces of woven silk done on a handloom, recreating the richness of eighteenth century brocades. The 'Fritillary' design is one of the largest samples of Garnett's work still known to be in existence with an orange, green and white colour-way in the Victoria and Albert Museum and a lilac, green and white combination in Abbot Hall in Kendal. Although no direct reference is made to this work in her diary, it was to be one of many royal orders. The first indication in the diary that the Queen was a regular customer was made in February and August of 1904; once when it was suggested that Garnett use this as a trade reference and then when noting a letter 'from Miss Knollys saying the Queen is keeping 20 yards of the silk and the account has this time to go in to H. M. Dresser and Wardrobe Woman, Miss Adams'.

Garnett's reputation, as alluded to in the citation at the beginning of this chapter, was not simply one for producing embroideries, dress or soft furnishing materials but also for hangings. In the absence of any colour photographs of these larger pieces it is indeed fortunate that Garnett, herself, recorded a description of a piece created to hang in an art gallery. The subject was the scene of an Italian sunset designed by the multi-media artist George Haité, sometime President of the Society of Designers and son of a well-known Paisley textile designer.[53] The work was commissioned by The Princess Louise School and in appointing Garnett, their manageress, Miss Symonds, related that 'they have been looking for materials to make it for the last three years'. In carrying out the work Garnett wrote:

> Now I am the proud maker of all the material to be used in it. The material is to be appliqué on a background which will be entirely covered, and every bit in it I have designed from Nature; from the glorious golden sunset woven on a yellow linen warp with weft of red silk and pure gold or of dull yellow and a brownish shade and gold in the darker parts; from the sun of pure gold to the lights and shades in the poplars and the olive groves, water, rocks and building I have caught the idea mostly from my favourite walk 'over the top' where Mike [her dog] and I have tramped together many times and watched the sun set and the fir trees take up their deepest shadows. The rocks in the foreground I have woven of coarse wool and linen; the tree trunks are all coarse linen; the near trees coarse throwan; distant ones and distant building fine throwan; whilst the mountains are fine linen in different mixtures; and the water is fine throwan; by this arrangement of material I think the different distances will be well preserved. The curtain when done measures ... 15 feet x 10 feet. Each piece is to be joined by braids; this part of it is to be done up in town under the direction of the Artist ...[54]

She finished the entry with a note of trepidation; 'I have done my part and await the verdict with some anxiety ...'. Unfortunately no reaction was recorded but Garnett clearly missed the involvement with this creation and wrote; 'I am sorry this piece of work is done; getting natural effects in the material is always full of interest … [but] I little thought I would ever be called on to design materials for a landscape picture'. She also recorded how she missed the effect of the bright colours of the original painting, which had hung on the workshop wall as her source of inspiration, so before returning it she made her own version: 'Copied Haité's picture and had to literally pile on paint to get anything like the effect …'.[55] Garnett's own ability in using her textiles to create such an artistic effect says much to challenge those who sought to separate art from craft and instead endorses the more holistic notion of creativity associated with the Arts and Crafts Movement.

In 1912 the publication of *Spinnery Notes* marked a new development with the opening of The New Spinnery opposite the village school with easier access for visitors to Bowness. This was to be an additional facility to the building at Fairfield and provided more space to display textiles, teach spinning, weaving and embroidery, and show the tools and equipment Garnett had collected in connection with her craft. As she wrote:

> Here, too will be the little museum where antiquities connected with spinning, weaving, embroidery, and other handicrafts will serve to show the continuity of these things from prehistoric times to the present day. The collection is, as yet, very small, but even so has taken many years to gather together.[56]

This development was, however, to be short lived. With the outbreak of the First World War Garnett closed the New Spinnery and

The New Spinnery in Bowness, which opened in 1912 but closed at the outbreak of World War One.

commercial production at The Spinnery ceased as it became the headquarters for the Windermere War Supply Depot. Not surprisingly Annie Garnett's name was not amongst those exhibiting at the 1916 Arts and Crafts Exhibition Society although she was still listed as a member. As for many others, the interruption of the war was to prove a significant economic as well as social factor in the continuity of this industry.

Post-War

For most of the early years after the war Garnett's role as 'Honorary Censor and Secretary of the War Depot', as well as her work with the Red Cross, seemed to involve her with much correspondence in the reallocation of surplus funds, materials and tools from the Depot. Acknowledgement of her war-time work was made with an invitation to a Royal Garden Party at Buckingham Palace in 1919 and a post-war certificate, 'In recognition of Admirable work done for our sailors and soldiers in all parts of the world'. However, it seems likely that as well as producing and sending bandages and splints abroad during the war, Annie Garnett did not completely give up her own weaving work. By 1920 there is an indication of a return to full production when in response to a request for photographs of her work, to be included in Paulson Townsend's 'Modern English Decorative Art', she replied; 'Unfortunately I have no photographs of anything done during the last few years ... During the war I purposely kept much of my work in abeyance but we are getting into full work again'.[57]

In seeking support for her business Garnett began corresponding with the various quangos, which had been set up by the Government to help rural industries re-establish themselves. This was to include a number of letters to the Director of Rural Industries, who had previously held the post of Secretary of the Rural League with responsibility for British Village Industries. One of his representatives was to call at The Spinnery and in writing to thank her for his copy of *Spinnery Notes* he added '... [I] greatly admire your aim and ideal, and hope it will meet with the success it fully deserves. I shall make known your work, as [I believe] that it will be an inspiration to many others'.

Despite this endorsement Garnett was bewildered to discover a year later that this same quango intended to offer money in support of a local branch of the Women's Institute, to start up a similar enterprise to the one at The Spinnery. This, as she wrote to the Director, Mr Green, at a time when '... most of my spinsters are idle now because of the times and for more than 6 months I have kept the looms going without a single order'. His response was defensive and informed her that the Rural Industries were to close down with the loss of his own employment. The postcard on which he wrote this has been torn in two, and perhaps says more than words to indicate the frustration Garnett must have felt in this situation. She did, however, persevere, this time with the Rural Industries Intelligence Bureau who were as they wrote;

> ... established under a Trust Deed for the purpose of assisting rural workers who, in their isolation are often out of touch with recent trade and economic information. In conjunction with the Bureau a Trading Society, known as the Country Industries Co-operative Society Limited, has been registered under the Industrial and Provident Societies Act, its function will be to supply the workers with raw materials at wholesale prices, and, if necessary, market their products for them.[58]

They in turn requested information on both The Spinnery and her knowledge of any competent instructors. This request reflects not only the lack of co-ordinated information but a failure to fully comprehend the nature of her business, a situation complicated possibly because of both the pre-war commercial and philanthropic elements of her work. Correspondence from The Women's Advisory Committee of the Bureau reveals a request for Garnett's opinion regarding the suitability of spinning as employment for disabled nurses and unemployed women. In responding she reveals something of the workings of The Spinnery in 1923 when replying:

> The whole question of price rests on the possibility of output I am afraid; one ought to be able to get back what one has paid a spinster for the yarn of fabric. Here I lend my wheels free; give the yarns out weekly, or whenever they need it: if it is coarsely spun they get less: if finely spun more: otherwise[?] is a delicate point: a bobbin is not always the same throughout: this may be a matter of temperament or of health, or merely carelessness – hand-spinning is human, literally lives: one just has to treat one's spinsters in a humane way and pay as much as even the selling price – the price made up without profit, will permit ...

This information was conveyed on the now utilitarian headed note-paper which bore her initials, no longer embellished but simply a straightforward capital A and G. Under the name of 'The Windermere Industry at The Spinnery' the hours of business were stated as 10 to 6.30, in the summer and in winter 10 to 4. A printed list of her products revealed hand-made textiles which included 'Silks, Brocades, Damasks, Samites of Gold, Throwans, Linens, Tweeds etc.' as well as 'Household Linen, Embroideries, Commenced Work'.[59]

When information for the Census of Production Papers for the Board of Trade (which had been addressed to Mr A Garnett) was completed for the year ending 1924, and sent to her Manchester accountant, it revealed stocks of silk, textiles made from silk and cotton mixes, silk and wool, silk and linen as well as pure wool to the net selling value of £1984. Materials used were valued at £1058. Wage earners throughout the year averaged out as just two males and three females, with between one and four outworkers. Machines in use were listed as one hand warping, many spinning wheels and eight handlooms.[60]

At around this time Annie Garnett suffered from some unknown illness and it was recorded that Hugh MacKay, an actor with the Arts League of Service, sang unaccompanied weaving and spinning songs to her, from the garden under her window, as she lay in her sick-bed. In a subsequent letter, to her, he referred to a weaver friend from the Orkneys who was looking for employment and whom he considered might be suitable for The Spinnery. This reference might bear some relation to the significant loss Annie Garnett must have felt when her head and longest serving weaver, Arthur Astle, was killed by a car outside St John's Church in Windermere. Whether Garnett, then in her sixties, took up the offer to employ another weaver is not known.

Annie Garnett and her sister Frances standing at the entrance to their lifelong home at Fairfield.

It is clear, however, that the peak years of her business had been synonymous with those of the Arts and Crafts Movement when individuality and creativity had flourished in rural workrooms. The autocratic way in which Annie Garnett had run The Spinnery at Bowness did not allow for any mediation on standards or a devolving of her authority through an heir apparent. Its success and ultimately its decline were due to the personal nature of her management which had found a sympathetic and conducive economic market in the pre-war context. Her correspondence, with a number of post-war rural support systems, reveals her persistence in trying to gain assistance for her business as an employer of local craft-workers. One is left to speculate as to whether this was because she no longer felt inspired to create the designs which had previously made her business financially viable or simply that she recognised the market for her exclusive textiles had dwindled. Despite the number of people associated with The Spinnery, its life-span and the textiles produced by this rural industry were to remain inextricably dependent on the energy and talents of one woman.

In conclusion

In this account I have tried, where possible, to provide information on the people who worked at, and supplied, The Spinnery but in the absence of documented business records this has relied on the presence of names in catalogues, newspaper accounts and personal writings. However, while the incomplete and fragmentary nature of the archive may itself have contributed to how this industry is perceived, the samples that remain bear witness to the range and sophistication of the products of this one-time textile industry at Bowness. The central character Annie Garnett is indeed worthy of further attention than this anthology allows.[61] No account can end, however, without saying more, albeit briefly, about two other passions in her life which in turn contributed to her creativity. Music, in keeping with her religious beliefs, she believed to be 'A Divine gift' and it provided her with both a deeply personal and social outlet.[62] In playing the cello, she received tuition in both Bowness and Liverpool. Her participation in the local orchestra was indeed significant as this short article from the *Westmorland Gazette* testified on 1 November 1924:

> *Miss Garnett's orchestra* – The weekly practices for this orchestra were resumed on Monday evening, the conductor being Mr Hubert Somervell of Kendal. In order to make the orchestra more complete, it is necessary to have many more wind instruments in it, and Miss Garnett of Fairfield Windermere will be glad to hear of anyone wishing to attend.

Her interest took her to the Leeds Festival of Music, as the guest of the Lord Mayor, to London and to the Wagnerian festival at Bayreuth. So moved was she by one performance she recorded 'I hope I may end my existence in a great wave of music'.[63]

Another passion was gardening and in 1907 she began the landscaping of the three acre garden at Fairfield. Detailed plans of which record how during the First World War it was utilised in providing food for the war effort and the selling of plants and seeds became another branch of her entrepreneurial work at The Spinnery. In 1930 Mary Lois Kissell wrote glowingly in the American magazine *Home Beautiful* of the many features and plants in the garden at Fairfield of which she claimed, 'Words seem inadequate when interpreting so astute a handling of color …'. Under the headline 'An Artist's Garden, A Color Laboratory in the English Lake Region' she wrote, 'It is with the freedom of a painter laying on pigment that Miss Garnett manipulates her medium of polychromatic flora, often most ingeniously massing tints and shades'. She observed how Garnett had used this palette;

> Not only was it a source of pleasure but the impressions caught in midday sun, glittering moonlight, morning mist, or heavy shower she transferred to weavings and embroideries in her workshop, 'The Spinnery'. Ere the opening of the twentieth century these inspirations were finding expression in both English and Scotch furnishing and clothing.[64]

During her working lifetime Garnett's artistic and skilled talents had been recognised with the membership of organisations like The Arts and Crafts Exhibition Society, The Home Arts and Industries Association, the Society of Women Artists and the esteemed Silk Association. She had employed over a hundred workers in the spinning and weaving of the textiles and threads, which had been produced in Bowness in a period of over thirty years. Her death in May 1942 warranted sadly only two modest lines in the *Westmorland Gazette.* There were no words to record her entrepreneurial and creative talents and there was no mention of a time when, as *The Studio* recorded in 1902, The Spinnery produced '… some of the most beautiful fabrics now made in this country'.

Acknowledgements

I am indebted to and thank the Pasold Fund for supporting my on-going research into the work of Annie Garnett. May I extend personal thanks to Mary Rose, Linda Parry, to the staff at Abbot Hall in Kendal and Gill Medland.

All photographs in this Chapter reproduced by kind permission of the Museum of Lakeland Life, Abbot Hall, Kendal, Cumbria.

Notes

1. *The Times*, 24 October 1906.
2. Anthea Callen, 'Sexual Division of Labour in the Arts and Crafts Movement' in Attfield and Kirkham (eds), *A View from the Interior, Women and Design* (The Women's Press, 1995), p. 151.
3. Lynne Walker, 'The Arts and Crafts Alternative' in ibid., p. 165.
4. Crawford (ed.), *By Hammer and Hand* (Birmingham Museums and Art Gallery, 1984), p. 17.
5. See Carolyn Heilbrun, *The Garnett Family* (Allen & Unwin, 1961) with sadly little information on the Lakeland branch.
6. J. Marshall, *Old Lakeland* (David & Charles, 1971), p. 172.
7. A. Garnett, unpublished diary 1899–1909, 22 January 1900.
8. *The Art Journal*, 1861, 1872, 1896 and 1897.
9. A. Callen, *Angel in the Studio* (Astragal Books, 1979), p. 24.
10. As expressed in advice to future craft-women in a letter to 'Mrs Glazebrook' on 10 December 1903 and recorded in her unpublished diary. It continued '... to observe nature: to cultivate a sympathy with nature; to read beautiful books; to think beautiful things; to be taught to draw; to express in given limits what she has observed of the growth of a leaf or flower.'
11. See Oliver Westall's account, 'The Retreat to Arcadia: Windermere as a Select Residential Resort in the Late Nineteenth Century' in Westall (ed.), *Windermere in the Nineteenth Century* (CNWRS, Lancaster, 1991), pp. 34 –48.
12. This diary which was later bound and embossed with the inscription 'Diary June 23rd to July 7th 1888' was illustrated and clearly meant for a more public viewing than the other diary referred to in this account.
13. Unpublished diary, 11 July 1899.
14. St Martin's Order book for the Langdale Linen Industry in Kendal Record Office. It states she bought three yards of linen at a cost of 3*s.* 6*d.* and that a bill for 10*s.* 10 ½ d. (approx. 55p) was settled ten days later on 22 July.
15. A. Garnett, *Spinnery Notes* (Chiswick Press, 1912), p. 11.
16. Unpublished diary, 11 July 1899.
17. A. Garnett, *Notes on Handspinning* (Dulau & Co., 1896), p. 13.
18. A. Garnett, unpublished diary, July 1899.
19. Ibid.
20. 'Art and Industry. Old-Time Spinning and Weaving in Lakeland' in *The Co-operative News*, 4 September (1909), p. 151.
21. Unpublished diary, 11 July 1899.
22. A. Garnett, article first published in the *Lyceum Club Magazine* and then later as a pamphlet entitled *Craftsmanship* in 1904.
23. Unpublished diary, 1 January 1900.
24. Ibid.
25. Ibid., January 1901.
26. Ibid., 30 September 1899.

27. Ibid., 23 September 1899.
28. Frances Garnett, on the occasion of the exhibition of Victorian and Edwardian Decorative Arts held at The Victora & Albert Museum in 1952 when three pieces of Annie Garnett's work were displayed. Described in the catalogue as: 'A hand-woven linen embroidered in silk and gold thread (V11), a stole, hand-woven silk damask (Y14) and a fragment, silk and silver-thread tissue (samite) (Y15)'.
29. Unpublished diary, 14 July 1899.
30. Ibid., 21 July 1899.
31. Ibid., 29 July 1899.
32. Ibid.
33. *Art Workers' Quarterly* (1905), p. 143.
34. Unpublished diary, 10 September 1900.
35. Gill Medland's dissertation 'Annie Garnett' submitted to Manchester Polytechnic, Dept. of General Studies for a B.A. (History of Design) May 1979 contains a wealth of technical information and is a key document in the archive. Gill's initial cataloguing of the archive made the exhibition of Annie Garnett's work at Abbot Hall in 1983 possible.
36. Unpublished diary, 12 December 1900.
37. *Art Workers' Quarterly* (1905), p. 143.
38. See chapter 4 on the Keswick School of Industrial Arts for more details.
39. Review in *The House*, February 1898.
40. Unpublished diary, 8 September 1900. Collections of the *Yule Tide Gift Catalogue* produced by Liberty & Co. Ltd are on micro-film in the National Art Library.
41. Unpublished diary, 15 May 1901. 'Harold Rathbone, a pupil of Ford Madox Brown, ran the della Robbia Pottery in Birkenhead ...' see A. Crawford (ed.), *By Hammer and Hand* (Birmingham Museum and Art Gallery, 1984), p. 39.
42. Unpublished diary, 24 February 1904.
43. Ibid., 28 October 1903.
44. Linda Parry, *Textiles of the Arts and Crafts Movement* (Thames and Hudson, 1988), p. 128.
45. A blue samite, again by Astle, was exhibited in 1910 and priced at £2 12*s*. 6*d*. See both the work of Garnett and Grasett in *Catalogue of the 9th Exhibition, Arts and Crafts Society* (Chiswick Press, 1910), items 407 and 419h.
46. Letter in the Garnett archive ref. 75/69/6/51.
47. Unpublished diary, 18 May 1901.
48. Ibid., 28 June 1901.
49. Ibid., 14 January 1901.
50. J. Marshall, *Old Lakeland* (David & Charles, 1971), p. 179.
51. Letter in the Garnett archive ref. 75/69/6/212. Reference to Lady Bective in unpublished diary, 19 November 1900.
52. A. Callen, *Angel in the Studio*, p. 99.
53. See Linda Parry, *Textiles of the Arts and Crafts Movement*, p. 126 for more details.

54. Unpublished diary, September 1900.
55. Ibid., 10 September 1900.
56. A. Garnett, *Spinnery Notes*, p. 14.
57. Correspondence in Garnett archive ref. 75/69/6/204.
58. Ibid., 75/69/6/21.
59. Ibid., 75/69/6/196.
60. Ibid., 75/69/6/216.
61. See J. Brunton, 'Cultural Narratives and the Historical Subject: Annie Garnett, her Diary, Life and Works', Ph.D. thesis, Lancaster University, 1999.
62. Unpublished diary, July 1899.
63. Ibid., 21 June 1900.
64. Kissell, *Home Beautiful*, vol. lxvii, U.S.A., March 1930.

Endings and Beginnings: a personal postscript

My research into this regional aspect of the Arts and Crafts Movement began over ten years ago when I first saw and became interested in the work of Annie Garnett. As a student on a City and Guild course attempting to sell my own creative embroidery I wanted to know how, at a time when women were perceived stereotypically to be confined within a domestic role, this nineteenth-century woman had managed to transfer her skills into a successful business. Getting to know Annie Garnett, through her personal writings, became intrinsic in understanding how she had negotiated the social nuances while managing the industry and maintaining a notion of respectability in the small provincial town of Bowness. The inspiration for her business, as I was to learn from her diary, had come from the Langdale Linen Industry and her visit to the 'little spinning home at Elterwater'; inevitably this led to a new area of research to find out what was happening there. The chapter in this book on the work at Langdale, while echoing some of the findings already published in *A History of Linen in the North West*,[1] bears witness to the fact that no history can ever be perceived as complete. This is perhaps especially true when research depends not on a neatly catalogued archive but on the fragmented collections families have passed on, and dim and distant personal memories informed by ageing photographs and newspaper cuttings.

Researching the Langdale Linen Industry, and identifying the key people involved, brought me into contact with Albert Fleming and Marion Twelves. Fleming's role as one of the instigators of the scheme is comparatively well documented but what of Twelves? Did she come to the Langdales to be his housekeeper and why did she really leave to go to Keswick? I have read and reproduced what Hardwicke Rawnsley wrote about her reason in wanting to continue her good work in Cumberland, and I have seen her own article in an American magazine, but will we ever really know why they appeared to fall-out and she moved away from the Langdales? Following the trail of Marion Twelves led me to the Keswick School of Industrial Arts and to tracing the work begun by Canon Rawnsley and his wife Edith in the parish of Wray. The classes in Keswick, however, reached new levels of expertise when trained designers were brought in, to teach at the school. Amongst one of the first had been Harold Stabler, a significant but under-researched figure, who learnt his initial skills under the auspices of Arthur W. Simpson and the Art School in Kendal. Simpson's social class and traditional training as a woodcarver may have appeared to mark him apart from the founders of the other regional industries, whose motivation was initiated by somewhat more philanthropic social ideas but, as I was to learn, his teaching, skills and enthusiasm transgressed any barriers to make him a key figure within this network.

No social or historical study, however, can relate to people without discussing the context in which their lives and work are enacted. The nineteenth century was dominated by the social and economic consequences of the increasing industrialisation of manufacture and commercial progress. Although, as has been discussed, the individual backgrounds of the key figures differed they were united in their abhorrence of this so-called progress which they saw as devaluing the notion of individual creativity and skill in the name of mass-production and profit. In articulating his opposition to such changes John Ruskin's words were central to what became known as The Arts and Crafts Movement, which had both an aesthetic and social agenda. Ruskin's reassertion of the artistic skill of the craft-worker challenged the elitist world of 'Fine Art' and advocated the essential importance of creativity to every individual. His rhetorical programme for social change was both revolutionary and reactionary but stressed the importance of a society rooted to the land and not the newly formed conurbations. His presence in the Lake District gave his ideas a regional association and provided opportunity for a more personal contact with those intent on putting his ideas into practice.

Conditions in the late nineteenth-century Lake District allowed all four industries access to an increasing tourist market as well as the growing number of retired and wealthy residents. As we have seen, Arthur W. Simpson and his firm were involved in woodcarving commissions in important houses built locally under the aesthetic influence of the Movement as well as supplying furniture to a wider market. Besides establishing a local clientele and selling smaller items through his shops to the visitors of Windermere and Kendal, Simpson's firm, like the other three industries, gained national and international recognition through exhibitions and competitions. His school at Gill Head brought together students and fellow-workers as revealed in the Visitors' Book. To see the signatures of Annie Garnett, her sister and sister-in-law together with the owner of Blackwell, Mrs Holt, provides a glimpse into a social world where workers and patrons mingled in their shared interest of retaining traditional craft-work. It was a world shattered by the outbreak of the First World War when people were touched by personal and economic devastation.

While the process of recovery, in the post-war years, for the industries discussed here was largely dictated to by wider economic conditions, the very nature of such enterprises is dependent on the individual resources and circumstances of their managers. Arthur W. Simpson relinquished control of his business to his son Hubert, a furniture maker who was to develop his own distinctive style while maintaining commissions for woodcarving. The marketplace, however, had changed and finding a footing for traditional rural-based craft work challenged the resources of Annie Garnett, as the correspondence discussed in the previous chapter reveals. Mrs Pepper, perhaps in today's speak, rationalised the Langdale Linen Industry continuing to produce smaller items and passing on her skills to those who were interested. The work at Keswick, with its mandate to teach and train continued beyond the life-time of its founders, including the indomitable Canon Rawnsley who died in 1920. It was not until 1984 that what had been the Keswick School of Industrial Arts finally ceased trading.

Today, buildings that once housed the creative output of those affiliated to the Arts and Crafts Movement provide holiday accommodation and sustenance to the Lakeland visitor. The items produced there, however, have proved a lasting legacy and once more have found an appreciative audience reflected not only in terms of the substantial sums paid at auctions but in the attention that they warrant as museum pieces. The purpose of this book has been to recapture the regional significance that a national Arts and Crafts Movement had on the Lake District and to reveal something of the people who participated so contributing locally, nationally and internationally to the transient success of this Movement.

Notes

1. Jennie Brunton, 'The late nineteenth-century revival of the Langdale linen industry', in Elizabeth Roberts (ed.), *A History of Linen in the North West* (CNWRS, 1998).

Index

Occasional Papers from the Centre for North-West Regional Studies

The Centre for North-West Regional Studies, based at Lancaster University, brings together members of the university and the regional community. As well as its extensive publication programme of books and resourse papers, it organises conferences, study days and seminars covering a wide range of subjects. For a small annual subscription 'Friends of the Centre' receive regular mailings of events and discounts on books and other activities.

For further details contact Centre for North-West Regional Studies, Fylde College, Lancaster University, Lancaster, LA1 4YF; tel: 01524 593770; fax: 01524 594725; email: christine.wilkinson@lancaster.ac.uk; Web site: www.lancs.ac.uk/users/cnwrs.

Irish Women in Lancashire, 2001, Sharon Lambert £9.95
Hadrian's Wall: A Social and Cultural History, 2000, Alison Ewin £8.50
Furness Abbey: Romance, Scholarship and Culture, 2000, C. Dade-Robertson £11.50
Rural Industries of the Lune Valley, 2000, Michael Winstanley £9.95
The Romans at Ribchester, 2000, B. J. N. Edwards £8.95
The Buildings of Georgian Lancaster (revised edition), 2000, Andrew White £6.95
A History of Linen in the North West, 1998, ed. Elizabeth Roberts £6.95
History of Catholicism in the Furness Peninsula, 1998, Anne C. Parkinson £6.95
Vikings in the North West – The Artifacts, 1998, B. J. N. Edwards £6.95
Sharpe, Paley and Austin, A Lancaster Architectural Practice 1836–1952, 1998, James Price £6.95
Romans and Britons in Northern England (revised edition), 1997, David Shotter £6.95
Victorian Terraced Housing in Lancaster, 1996, Andrew White and Mike Winstanley £6.95
Walking Roman Roads in the Fylde and the Ribble Valley, 1996, Philip Graystone £5.95
Romans in Lunesdale, 1995, David Shotter and Andrew White £6.50
Roman Route Across the Northern Lake District, Brougham to Moresby, 1994, Martin Allan £5.95
Walking Roman Roads – East Cumbria, 1994, Philip Graystone £5.95
St Martin's College, Lancaster, 1964–89, 1993, Peter S. Gedge and Lois M. R. Louden £5.95
From Lancaster to the Lakes: the Region in Literature, 1992, eds Keith Hanley and Alison Millbank £5.95
Windermere in the Nineteenth Century, 1991, ed. Oliver M. Westall £4.95
Grand Fashionable Nights: Kendal Theatre, 1989, Margaret Eddershaw £3.95
Rural Life in South West Lancashire, 1988, Alistair Mutch £3.95
The Diary of William Fisher of Barrow, 1986, eds William Rollinson and Brett Harrison £2.95
Richard Marsden and the Preston Chartists, 1981, J. E. King £2.95

Each of these titles may be ordered by post from the above address, postage and packing £1.00 per order. Please make cheques payable to 'The University of Lancaster'. Titles are also available from all good booksellers in the region.